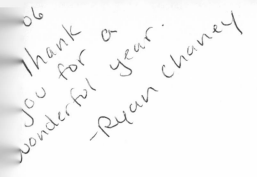

06

Thank you for a wonderful year.

-Ryan Chaney

The Future of
the United Nations

The Future of
the United Nations

Understanding the Past
to Chart a Way Forward

Joshua Muravchik

The AEI Press

Publisher for the American Enterprise Institute

WASHINGTON, D.C.

Available in the United States from the AEI Press, c/o Client Distribution Services, 193 Edwards Drive, Jackson, TN 38301. To order, call toll free: 1-800-343-4499. Distributed outside the United States by arrangement with Eurospan, 3 Henrietta Street, London WC2E 8LU, England.

Library of Congress Cataloging-in-Publication Data
Muravchik, Joshua
   The future of the United Nations : understanding the past to chart a way forward / Joshua Muravchik.
      p. cm.
   Includes bibliographical references and index.
   ISBN 0-8447-7183-X (alk. paper)
1. United Nations—History. 2. United Nations. I. Title.

   JZ4984.5.M87 2005
   341.23'09--dc22

                                                    2005019447

10 09 08 07 06 05   1 2 3 4 5 6 7

Cover photograph caption: USA, New York, United Nations Building

Printed in the United States of America

Contents

ACKNOWLEDGMENTS   vii

INTRODUCTION   1

1. THE BIRTH OF THE UN: A CASE OF THOUGHTLESS
   PATERNITY   7

2. AFTER SIXTY YEARS: FAILURE ON MANY FRONTS   17
   Keeping the Peace   17
   Nuclear Nonproliferation   34
   A Moral Beacon?   42
   Human Rights   59
   Some Nations Are Less Equal than Others   62
   Combating Poverty   69

3. SOME AREAS OF SUCCESS   73
   Peacekeeping   73
   Regulatory Agencies   75

4. SOURCES OF FAILURE   81
   The Non-Aligned Movement   81
   European Anti-Americanism   83
   Lack of Accountability   86
   Serving Its Own Interests   89

5. PROPOSALS FOR REFORM: HOPE SPRINGS ETERNAL   92
   Improving the UN's Efficiency   94
   Enhancing the UN's Capabilities   97

Revising the UN's Political Structures *100*
The Security Council and the United States *106*

6. A BETTER APPROACH   110

APPENDIX A: WHICH UNITED NATIONS MEMBER
COUNTRIES VOTED MOST OFTEN WITH THE
UNITED STATES IN THE UN GENERAL ASSEMBLY?   123

APPENDIX B: ODD MAN OUT OR BACK WHERE
WE STARTED?   129

APPENDIX C: THE UN'S BUDGET: WHO PAYS?   130

APPENDIX D: THE COMMISSION ON HUMAN
RIGHTS: FOXES GUARDING THE CHICKEN COOP   136

NOTES   139

INDEX   155

ABOUT THE AUTHOR   167

Acknowledgments

I am indebted to Jeane Kirkpatrick, my friend and mentor, who performed so brilliantly as the permanent representative of the United States to the United Nations, for sharing with me her illuminating insights into the UN. Two other friends were extremely helpful to me. Mark Lagon, the deputy assistant secretary of state for international organizations, repeatedly took time from his busy schedule to explain to me various details about how the UN works and to give me the benefit of his own acute observations. Amanda Schnetzer consented to do a piece of research for me, which she executed with the diligence and high degree of intelligence that are her trademarks. I am most grateful, too, to my extremely talented research assistant, Suzanne Gershowitz, and to three other outstanding staff members who assisted me at various stages of the project: Vance Serchuk, Assia Dosseva, and Kara Nichols Barrett. I also received valuable assistance from several unusually capable interns: Tobias Harris, Mario Loyola, Sebastian Seedorf, Matthew Lange-Geise, Ronald Docksai, Melanie Meerschwam, Yonit Golub, Yonina Alexander, and Moses Sternstein. Last but far from least, I owe thanks to Chris DeMuth and the other officers and trustees of AEI for their support of my research and for providing such a conducive environment in which to do it.

Introduction

After sixty years, the United Nations, as we know it, is a failure. It stands as a monument to naïve American idealism. American idealism has done some great things for the world: It spurred the end of colonialism, the rise of human rights, and the spread of democracy. But it has sometimes gone off the rails, as in 1928, when the United States foisted on the world the Pact of Paris that "outlawed" war. Or in 1945, when the United States persuaded the other nations that the way "to save succeeding generations from the scourge of war," as the preamble of the UN charter expressed it, was to build a new international organization on the ashes of that earlier American brainchild, the League of Nations, which had failed so utterly to forestall World War II.

The UN was unable from the start to prevent the Cold War. Indeed, it might be said the Cold War had already begun as early as the summer of 1944, when the Red Army abetted the Nazis in destroying the Polish Home Army so as to clear obstacles to the creation of a postwar Soviet empire in Europe.[1] But the Americans, busy building their dream castles of peace, did not recognize the implications of this event until some years later.

When they finally faced the facts, the Americans fought back with characteristic effectiveness, and the UN was thrown into gridlock by the stalemate between Washington and Moscow. There it remained until after the Berlin Wall came down, consecrating the Kremlin's decision to call off the contest.

This made it possible for the UN to break free. In 1990, when Iraq invaded Kuwait, President George H. W. Bush opted to take the matter to the Security Council even before he brought it to

Congress. The remarkable reason for this was that once he concluded that the liberation of Kuwait would require the use of force, he knew it would be easier to win the assent of the Soviet Union, China, France, and Britain than of Democrats in Congress. Only with the Security Council's endorsement in hand was he able to secure a narrow majority in the Senate.

As a result of this experience, Bush's administration left office proclaiming high hopes for the UN, which, it said, had "been given a new lease on life, emerging as a central instrument for the . . . preservation of peace."[2] Succeeding Bush, President Bill Clinton took a still more hopeful view. Convinced that "we've simply got to focus on rebuilding America," Clinton declared his intention to rely more on the world body to handle international problems.[3] "U.N. peacekeeping holds the promise to resolve many of this era's conflicts," he said, and his first UN ambassador, Madeleine Albright, envisioned "assertive multilateralism" as a cornerstone of U.S. policy and world peace.[4]

The UN secretary general, Boutros Boutros-Ghali of Egypt, saw in this post–Cold War American attitude an "extraordinary opportunity to expand, adapt, and reinvigorate the work of the United Nations."[5] His deputy, Undersecretary General Vladimir Petrovsky, said the goal was to create a "pax U.N."[6] But a string of disasters—Bosnia, Somalia, Rwanda—made hash of Clinton's high hopes, and by 1994 Albright was singing a different tune: "The one sentence summary of our policy is that it is not intended to expand UN peacekeeping, but to help fix it."[7]

While the United States was growing disenchanted with the UN, much of the world was growing wary of the United States. In the Cold War, American power had been seen by most as a welcome counterweight to Soviet power. But no one needed protection from a Soviet Union that no longer existed. Now it was America's own outsized power—not counterbalanced by any other force—that was disconcerting. While longtime enemies continued to decry the United States as the bastion of imperialism, Zionism, and Satan, or to warn against American "hegemony," America's traditional friends began to voice their own unease.

The popular German newsmagazine *Der Spiegel* put it, "Americans are acting, in the absence of limits put on them by anybody or anything, as if they own a blank check in their 'McWorld.'"[8] In a similar vein, Karl Lamers, the foreign policy spokesman for Germany's Christian Democrats (the party usually considered more pro-American), lamented: "I wouldn't want the Soviet Union back, but there's a counterweight missing."[9] All of this was in the 1990s—before Iraq, before Afghanistan, before the presidency of George W. Bush. The tool for reining in the United States that commended itself to these worriers was the UN. This approach first surfaced in European discourse in the mid-1990s about the possibility of "out-of-area" missions by NATO. Leaders of the French, German, Belgian, and Dutch governments, among others, said they opposed any military action, other than territorial self-defense, without a mandate from the Security Council.[10] For the French especially, the issue went far beyond NATO. Foreign Minister Hubert Vedrine called on his country to "drum up ad hoc majorities or blocking minorities" in order to counter "the overriding predominance of the United States." This, he explained, was the reason for "defending organized multilateralism and the requirements of the Security Council."[11]

Accordingly, when, in the aftermath of 9/11, the Bush administration made clear its unwillingness to tolerate Saddam Hussein's continued defiance of his disarmament obligations under the terms of the armistice that ended the 1991 Gulf War, French president Jacques Chirac feigned cooperation. In an interview with the *New York Times*, "Mr. Chirac proposed a Security Council resolution that would give Iraq a three-week deadline for admitting United Nations weapons inspectors 'without restrictions or preconditions.' If Mr. Hussein rejected their return or hampered their work, he said, a second resolution should be passed on whether to use military force."[12] Washington took the bait and came to terms on resolution 1441, finding Iraq in "material breach" of its disarmament obligations resulting from its 1990 aggression against Kuwait and offering it "a final opportunity to comply" or else face "serious consequences."[13]

When Iraq yielded only incomplete compliance, the United States brought the matter back to the Security Council, as Chirac had proposed. But then he sprang his trap, blocking any Security Council authorization of force with the threat of a French veto. Having gone back to the council, the United States found itself in the position that if it acted without French approval it laid itself open to the accusation that it was itself behaving roguishly.

President Bush went to war nonetheless, supported by what allies he could muster. This, in the eyes of many other members of the UN, was an egregious act of "unilateralism" and a defiance of the international system. Vedrine's successor, Foreign Minister Dominique de Villepin of France, led the outrage, crying that the "world order" had been "shattered" by America's action.[14] Even Secretary General Kofi Annan added his voice to those branding America's action "illegal."[15]

The latter accusation reflected the theory that the use of force, except to repulse an armed attack or at the behest of the UN Security Council, is illegitimate, since it is forbidden by the UN charter. This idea did not begin with the Iraq crisis. According to Deputy Secretary General Shashi Tharoor, "Several countries, from Norway to India, do not or cannot (as a matter of politics, policy, or constitutional law) commit forces overseas without the council's explicit authorization."[16] But such policies have often been honored in the breach. India did not consult the Security Council when it invaded and absorbed Goa in 1961, nor when it sent troops to separate what was then East Pakistan from West in 1971, creating Bangladesh. Norway took part in the 1999 NATO air war against Serbia over the issue of Kosovo, which did not have the approval of the council, nor could such approval have been secured due to the likelihood of a veto by Russia. (So, too, did France, Germany, and the other members of NATO.)

Moreover, such a strict construction of the UN charter has not always been upheld by all who propose it today. Consider the three permanent members of the Security Council who voiced opposition to the United States in regard to Iraq in 2003. France did not ask for UN approval in 1979 when its paratroopers toppled the regime of Jean-Bedel Bokassa in the Central African Empire. Russia sought the imprimatur of the UN for the forces it had deployed in some former Soviet republics, such as Georgia and Moldova—but did not receive it. Russia claimed that these forces served to keep the peace, and so they may have done; but they also served to maintain Russia's influence and support local Russians or other ethnic groups in resisting the authority of the central governments of those countries. Therefore, other members of the world body were unwilling to place the UN's seal on the Russia deployments. The troops were stationed nonetheless. China did not turn to the UN in 1979 before sending its troops into Vietnam to, as China's leader Deng Xiaoping put it, "teach Vietnam a lesson."[17]

What infused this principle with new urgency was the unprecedented situation of "unipolarity." For many, the debate over Iraq was not so much about Iraq as it was about the United States. As Tharoor put it, "The exercise of American power may well be the central issue in world politics today."[18]

So it may be. But the fear of American power (except on the part of violent miscreants or those who harbor the wish to be such) is misplaced. Mexico has a two-thousand-mile border with the United States; Canada's is four thousand miles long. Neither is defended. Both countries often oppose Washington's policies. And what price do they pay? As Canadian political scientist Alexander Moens quipped, "The dire result for our nation's leader seems to be another lunch at the ranch with President Bush."[19] In truth, the world has more to fear from America's old habit of isolationism than from any imperial temptation.

The world also has more to fear from the gambit of deploying the UN to stymie the United States. Until this point, politely overlooking the UN's conspicuous ineffectiveness seemed to be the better part of valor. Although the UN's record was disappointing, it remained the object of many hopes and affections. Today, however, the UN is being put forward as an alternative to what some see as an emerging *pax Americana*. If the alternative, the *pax UN*, were genuine, then there would be much to recommend it. But it is an illusion, and it could be a source of much harm.

This demands an unflinching assessment of the performance of the UN. Moreover, it demands that we think through ways that the

UN might be overhauled so as to magnify the good that it does and reduce the prospects for damage.

1

The Birth of the UN: A Case of Thoughtless Paternity

The anguished relations between the United States and the United Nations are ironic because the UN is largely an American invention, as was the very idea of a universal organization of states. Around the beginning of the twentieth century, America passed Britain as the world's largest economy, and the upstart nation began to emerge from its isolationist cocoon to find its place in world politics. That search has continued for over a hundred years now, with oscillations between globalism and isolationism. Meanwhile, the rest of the world has struggled to come to terms with the burgeoning American colossus. Much of this drama has revolved around international organizations.

In World War I, the United States made its grand entry onto the stage of international politics, sealing the war's outcome. After the armistice, President Woodrow Wilson set out to forge a lasting peace by bringing to birth a "new diplomacy" based on fairness and principle. Its cornerstone, as enunciated in Wilson's "Fourteen Points," would be "a general association of nations . . . formed under specific covenants for the purpose of affording mutual guarantees of political independence and territorial integrity to great and small states alike."

Most other governments were skeptical of this vision. But Washington possessed political capital in abundance—both from America's newly demonstrated military prowess and Wilson's pathbreaking appeal to European public opinion as he toured Europe on his way to Versailles for the peacemaking. The other world leaders swallowed their misgivings and yielded to many of

Wilson's novel demands, especially for the creation of the League of Nations, in return for American acquiescence in a variety of territorial claims and deals that cut against the grain of the president's famous Fourteen Points. But then Wilson lost his influence at home, and the United States, having persuaded, cajoled, and bribed the other states to form the League, refused to join it.

In the wake of World War II, America once again found itself in the leading position to shape the peace, and once again it made the creation of an international organization its chief goal. Indeed, this was pursued almost single-mindedly at the expense of other objectives, such as the freedom of Eastern Europe. At the Moscow conference of foreign ministers in October 1943, Britain's Anthony Eden, aiming to blunt the Kremlin's increasingly clear intent to dominate the nations on its periphery, proposed that the allies form a commission to settle postwar European issues. Naturally, the Soviet minister, Vyachislav Molotov, resisted any such constraint on Moscow's free hand. He was reinforced in this by none other than the U.S. secretary of state, Cordell Hull, "for whom," as Townsend Hoopes and Douglas Brinkley observed, "an overarching global organization was the first imperative, and who saw a threat to this in every regional idea."[1] To Hull, a European commission appeared a greater danger than Soviet expansionism.

Both the British and the Soviet leaders were skeptical of a new global organization. Roosevelt sought to bring Stalin around first. He used the occasion of the first wartime summit of the "Big Three," in Teheran in November 1943 for private meetings with the Soviet dictator in order to neutralize him, thus isolating Churchill.[2] The president's intense concentration on putting across an international organization continued into the next summit, at Yalta in February 1945. As Stephen Schlesinger put it, "There were other critical issues that Roosevelt was going to deal with at Yalta, but at the forefront of his mind was Stalin's cooperation on the U.N."[3]

The creation and design of an international organization were not matters of the first importance to Stalin, and he undoubtedly read the American president's eagerness as something he could exploit. Hoopes and Brinkley describe the underlying bargain that was reached at Yalta:

> To prevent a U.S. reversion to isolationism after the war, U.S. participation in a new world organization was the sine qua non, but the United Nations could not be brought into being without genuine Russian cooperation, and that depended on Western accommodation to unpalatable manifestations of the Soviet Communist system in Eastern Europe.[4]

The United States, in short, not only dreamed up the idea of the UN; it spent copiously of the diplomatic capital earned by the sacrifice of its sons in battle to bring it into being. Yet for most of the UN's history, the United States has had difficult relations with it, even while serving as host to the world body and bearing the largest share of its costs.

As if this were not irony enough, some of the features of the UN that give Washington the greatest trouble were explicitly insisted upon by the Americans. The Economic Social Council (ECOSOC), sponsor of many UN activities from which the United States has dissented, was created at America's insistence, based on the idea that to address the threat of war directly without also seeking to ameliorate its root causes would be insufficient.

Similarly, the UN Commission on Human Rights, where America so often finds itself outvoted at the behest of dictators, was also created under American leadership in the person of Eleanor Roosevelt. And the narrow definition of self-defense in article 51 of the UN charter, which critics say disallowed American actions in Iraq in 2003, was insisted upon by Secretary of State Edward Stettinius in the face of British foreign minister Anthony Eden's attempts to broaden it. The imputed Security Council monopoly on the legitimate use of force grew directly from President Roosevelt's plan that the peace of the postwar world would be upheld by "four policemen"—America, the Soviet Union, the United Kingdom, and China—who would exercise exclusive authority to resort to war.

For President Franklin Roosevelt and Prime Minister Winston Churchill, the UN was seen as the necessary antithesis to American isolationism. The League of Nations had been the centerpiece of President Wilson's global strategy, which had been America's first venture in internationalism. The Senate's rejection of the League and the country's return to isolationism in the 1920s and '30s were seen as two sides of the same coin. Roosevelt said that America's losses in World War I had gone "unredeemed" because of the country's failure to join the League, leading to World War II.[5]

The argument that American isolationism had helped pave the way to the second war was incontrovertible, but it may have been misfocused. As historians Douglas Brinkley and Townsend Hoopes have observed, "It is by no means certain that U.S. participation [in the League] would have prevented Hitler's coming to power, the progressive erosion of international stability in the 1930s or the ultimate cataclysm."[6] The necessary ingredient for facing up to Hitler earlier would have been courage, and the League was not a setting that evoked courage. In theory, its multilateral structure should have lent its members confidence, but in practice it only invited buck-passing and searches for the least common denominator. What was more likely to have worked was a firm U.S. commitment to the security of England and France, something those countries had wanted desperately. Such backing might well have fortified them to take the tough steps that only they could have taken to stop Hitler before he became too strong, when he first began violating the terms of the peace treaty. Indeed, the United States had made such a commitment at Versailles, but it was washed away when the Senate declined to approve the treaty.

The refusal of the United States to join the League may have had the effect of obscuring the organization's shortcomings. It was easy to attribute its failing to the vacuum created by the absence of the world's richest nation, and this was undoubtedly a critical weakness. But this obvious flaw deflected statesmen and analysts from considering whether the organization was defective in a deeper way, whether it would have functioned appreciably better had the American chair not been empty.

The fear that haunted internationalists, not least of them President Roosevelt, was that the end of the second war, like the end of the first, would be followed by a recrudescence of American isolationism. Because isolationism was so closely linked to rejection of the League, it was taken as axiomatic that keeping America engaged internationally after the war meant constructing a new international organization. Historian Robert Dallek wrote that to Roosevelt, "a United Nations would not only provide a vehicle for drawing Russia into extended cooperation with the West, but would also assure an initial American involvement in postwar affairs."[7]

Due perhaps to the assumption that a new international organization was the key to keeping the Senate or American public opinion from reverting to isolationism, there were few voices raised in the United States to suggest pursuing an internationalist policy by other means. This must be judged an astonishing intellectual failure on the part of the statesmen and thinkers of that era. The idea of international organization was new and novel. It had been tried once and failed. Most nations at most times, having had little choice, had pursued internationalist policies in other ways. The peace of Europe was maintained during most of the nineteenth century by the Concert of Europe, an informal mechanism, and by the balance-of-power policies of Britain toward the continent. The United States itself, in its one time-honored departure from isolationism, had a policy of hemispheric exclusion called the Monroe Doctrine. Could not America conduct an active foreign policy in the second half of the twentieth century by methods of statecraft such as these?

One of the few who raised such questions was the commentator Walter Lippmann. Lippmann argued that "an international order . . . can be established only by the coordinated action of groups of national states. One of these groups I venture to call the Atlantic Community, and since we belong to it, it must naturally be our first concern."[8]

In an adumbration of the theory of a "clash of civilizations" that was to be advanced by scholar Samuel Huntington half a century later, Lippmann foresaw other "strategical systems" or "constellations" grouped around Russia and China, and in the Hindu and Moslem worlds. Although typecast as a "realist," Lippmann put strong emphasis on democracy: "The great lasting commitments of the United States in the outer world are confirmed, in the last analysis, not by treaties and declarations but by the fact that they enlist the American democracy as the champion of democracy," he said.[9]

Yet Lippmann was strangely sanguine about what this portended for U.S. relations with the Soviet Union, observing that "since we became allies in war, the Soviet Union has been committing itself more and more definitively to a foreign policy based on democratic, and not totalitarian, principles."[10] The point about Lippmann is not that his vision was unclouded, but that almost alone he sought to grapple with the alternatives that might be available to the United States, while the bulk of his contemporaries fixed on the simple dichotomy of isolationism versus international organization.

One reason ideas such as Lippmann's were rarely heard was America's longstanding aversion to alliances. The country experienced its belated entry into the First World War in 1917 as a traumatic loss of innocence. Washington announced punctiliously that it was fighting as an "associated" power, not as a member of an alliance. Wilson denounced the secret deals that were considered normal among the wartime allies as inherently tawdry. The first of his famous "Fourteen Points" foreswore "private international understandings of any kind." In place of this "old diplomacy," he put forward the idea of "a general association of nations." He elaborated on this the next year in his "five particulars," which made clear that the "new diplomacy" would have no room for alliances: "There can be no leagues or alliances or special covenants and understandings within the general and common family of the League of Nations." It was this kind of thinking that led George Kennan to decry America's "legalistic-moralistic approach to international problems . . . the belief that it should be possible to suppress the chaotic and dangerous aspirations of governments in the international field by the acceptance of some system of legal rules and restraints."[11]

In the Second World War, America was less standoffish, at least after Pearl Harbor. It embedded itself unapologetically in an alliance—the United Nations, it was called. But in laying plans for what would follow the war, Washington's goal was to convert this alliance into an organization of the whole world.

British leaders went along with these plans, seeing them as the surest means of keeping America from turning inward once again. Although Churchill had pressed for an American commitment to a new international organization as early as his first wartime meeting with Roosevelt at Agentia in August 1941, there is evidence for doubting whether the British leader saw such a body as valuable in its own right. His main goal was to win a commitment that "the United States would join with us in policing the world" once the war was over.[12] His secretary of state for war, Anthony Eden, expressed the underlying view of the British government:

> Only by formation of some World Organization are we likely to induce the Americans, and this means the American Senate, to agree to accept any European commitments designed to range America, in case of need, against . . . any European breaker of the peace.[13]

London's key aim was to draw the United States into an alliance, much as the French had tried in vain to do during the 1920s. Whereas the founding of the UN was overwhelmingly an American-driven exercise, British foreign minister Ernest Bevin initiated what became the North Atlantic Treaty. This treaty—and the organization it gave rise to—was to keep the peace of Europe for the rest of the century while the UN remained, at most, a sideshow. Ironically, NATO—and not the UN—served also to inculcate in Americans a deep and enduring spirit of internationalism. This new spirit abided in the sense that we had partners who shared our values and were prepared to stand shoulder to shoulder with us in a dangerous world, that our safety was entwined with theirs, and that if worse came to worst we would fight in the same trench. It embedded an internationalist outlook into the American psyche more firmly than all the orotund speeches, solemn resolutions, and diplomatic pageantry of the General Assembly and Security Council.

When the UN was designed, some of the models circulated during the early deliberations in the State Department put greatest emphasis on regional organizations. These would have been the principal working bodies, with only occasional issues referred on a global basis to the great powers for consideration. Such an approach was strongly favored by Churchill, who argued that "Only the countries whose interests were directly affected by a dispute . . . could be expected to apply themselves with sufficient vigor to secure a settlement."[14] In the end, however, the charter made only minor allowance for regional organizations.

Article 52 recognizes "regional arrangements for dealing with . . . matters relating to the maintenance of international peace and security." This language has sometimes been invoked as authorization for the use of force, such as the American blockade of Cuba during the 1961 missile crisis, which was endorsed by the Organization of American States, the 1983 U.S. invasion of Grenada, which was undertaken in the name of the Organization of Eastern Caribbean States, and the 1998 NATO bombing campaign against Serbia in response to its actions in Kosovo. But such an argument flies in the face of article 53, which added this unambiguous qualifier to the rights granted in article 52: "No enforcement action shall be taken under regional arrangements or by regional agencies without the authorization of the Security Council."

Legal arguments aside, the important point is that the founders chose to base the organization on the twin pillars of the Security Council and the General Assembly rather than on regional structures. This was a triumph of idealism over realism, and for the principle of universality. It brought the UN a step closer to being the skeleton of a world government.

Lacking the element of direct national interest that Churchill argued was more likely to be present for members of regional organizations, the design of the UN presupposed some common values that would bind the members together. Indeed, the charter begins,

We the peoples of the United Nations determined to save succeeding generations from the scourge of war. . . and to

> reaffirm faith in fundamental human rights, in the dignity
> and worth of the human person, and in the equal rights
> of men and women and of nations large and small.

These values, it is evident, transcend or at least constrain the naked self-interest of states.

The charter then punctuates this sense of commonality by opening membership not to all, but rather to "peace-loving states." More specifically, a 1943 memo from Secretary of State Cordell Hull to President Roosevelt explained that "the entire plan" for the proposed organization was based

> on two central assumptions: First, that the four major
> powers [the United States, the United Kingdom, the
> Soviet Union, and China] will . . . consider themselves
> morally bound not to go to war against each other or
> against any other nation, and to cooperate with each
> other . . . in maintaining the peace; and Second, that each
> of them will maintain adequate forces and be willing to
> use such forces as circumstances require to prevent or
> suppress all cases of aggression.[15]

This illustrates not only the extremely hopeful, one might say naïve, assumptions that undergirded the UN, but also how much the founders were the prisoners of recent experience, painfully weak in their ability to imagine a future unlike the past. All the time the idea for the UN was being developed, the Roosevelt administration could scarcely envision any U.S. adversary other than a revived Germany or Japan, or any threat to the peace originating elsewhere.

This presupposition was, in turn, based on the premise that the Soviet Union would remain permanently cooperative, if not friendly, if only it could be drawn into an international organization. As Gaddis Smith notes, "Throughout most of the war President Roosevelt and his advisers worried less about the possibility of conflict with Russia than about the continued existence of western, particularly British, imperialism" which they believed was "far more likely to produce a third world war than anything that Russia might do."[16]

The wartime alliance had fostered illusions in the United States about the Soviet system. U.S. ambassador Joseph Davies was such an ardent admirer of Stalin's that he liked almost everything he saw in the Soviet Union. He even lent his imprimatur to the verdicts of the notorious show trials of the dictator's rivals, cabling home to the State Department his conclusion that the accused had been proven "beyond a reasonable doubt . . . guilty of treason."[17]

In contrast to the reviled fascists, the Soviet state was often portrayed as a fellow democracy, albeit a different kind of democracy. To the extent that American leaders suspected, despite the reports from their ambassador, that unsavory things went on within the Kremlin, they hoped that somehow the experience of wartime partnership would soften the Soviet regime. And even insofar as they harbored doubts about Soviet motives, they nourished the hope that the Soviets would feel their own need for peace and cooperation in order to recover from the war.

While American leaders were nursing such soothing thoughts, in the Kremlin, Stalin, thrilled by the drama of the earthshaking events of which he was a main pilot, told a visiting delegation of Yugoslav Communists excitedly that "the war shall soon be over. We shall recover in fifteen or twenty years, and then we'll have another go at it."[18] The entire design of the United Nations rested on the U.S. government's hopeless misreading of Soviet intentions.

2

After Sixty Years: Failure on Many Fronts

Keeping the Peace

How, then, sixty years after these inauspicious beginnings, does the UN stack up? First, let us consider its foremost purpose: the preservation of international peace and security. Chapter VII of the charter entrusts the Security Council with responding to "any threat to the peace, breach of the peace, or act of aggression" by deploying armed force "to maintain or restore international peace and security." Toward this end, this section also establishes a "Military Staff Committee" (MSC) and requires all member states to make units of their armed forces "available to the Security Council, on its call."

But this entire apparatus has been a dead letter almost from the start. Talks about how to implement it began soon after the UN's founding. For a year and a half, the American delegates earnestly proposed formulas for the size, composition, command, and basing of the UN military, but these fell on deaf ears, leading one of the Americans, General Matthew Ridgway, to report to General George Marshall that "the MSC has dogged along like a hound on a dusty country lane. You are sure by watching him that he has some purpose and distinction, though neither are apparent. He attracts little attention and the dust he raises quickly disappears."[1] Eventually, the impasse was referred to the Security Council, where it was not broken.

Thereafter, the Military Staff Committee was not dissolved. What happened instead was described vividly by the former Israeli ambassador to the UN, Abba Eban:

> The five generals and eight admirals of the military staff committee, brilliantly uniformed and bemedaled, would hold ritual meetings a few minutes long at the beginning of each month. The chairman would call them to order, announce that no speakers were scheduled, and propose adjournment. A new chairman would take office the next month according to alphabetical rotation.[2]

The impasse of the Military Staff Committee rendered nugatory the entire structure of peace envisioned in the charter. The nations were to entrust their security and the peace of the world to the UN. It, in turn, was to dispose a mighty army that would equip it to fulfill this supreme mission. But, suddenly, there was no army. Not a single troop or weapon. The nations stood naked before potential predators. The entire system was revealed to rest on illusory premises. What did the Security Council do to reconsider how, then, the UN might fulfill its bedrock "peace and security" function? It did nothing at all.

The problem with the UN's illusory peace machinery was not a matter only of its missing army. The problem began with the Security Council itself. The five permanent members, a derivation from Roosevelt's concept of the "four policemen," were entrusted with paramount responsibility for keeping the peace. But the composition itself was farcical. France, although defeated and powerless, was added to the four at Churchill's behest because it was Britain's longtime ally, and he was eager to see it built up again as a makeweight against Germany or Russia. China was added, not for any strength of its own, but as a gesture to the non-Western world. It was, however, riven by civil war, and its government was soon overthrown. The Soviet Union was a poor choice for a policeman, being itself a criminal state. Far from being "peace-loving," it had colluded with Hitler in launching the European war, in the process swallowing up the Baltic states and parts of Poland, Romania, and Finland. Now at war's end, even as it was assuming its seat on the Security Council, it was hungrily ingesting the rest of its neighbors, or attempting to do so. The United Kingdom, in contrast, was indeed a responsible member of the international community and devoted to peace, but it was a spent power, utterly drained from the war. In truth, then, there was only one policeman, so long as it was prepared to act the role: the United States.

Only twice in its sixty-year history has the Security Council authorized the use of force in response to a cross-border breach of the peace, the kind of depredation it was designed to prevent: in Korea in 1950 and in Kuwait in 1990. On neither occasion did it even make the pretense of acting under the articles of the charter (39, 42, 43) that spell out its responsibility to uphold the peace. Rather, on each occasion it acted under article 51, which reaffirms "the inherent right of individual or collective self-defense." In these cases, the council authorized other states to come to the aid of South Korea and Kuwait, respectively, in their pursuit of self-defense. But article 51 was explicitly framed as a stopgap to be invoked in emergencies "until the Security Council has taken measures necessary to maintain international peace and security." In other words, the Security Council has only succeeded in acting to defend the peace by means of the very provision designed for situations in which it is unable or fails to act. What a confession of impotence!

That the Security Council did act against North Korea's aggression was made possible only by the odd situation that the Soviet Union was absent. A few months earlier, Moscow had begun to boycott the council to protest the fact that Chiang Kai-shek's Nationalist government was still seated in China's chair, even though the Communists, led by Mao Zedong, had driven Chiang's government into exile and taken over as the rulers of the Chinese mainland. The Kremlin's tactic had the unintended consequence of preventing it from exercising its veto, as it surely would have done, when the council authorized countries to rally to the defense of South Korea.

As soon as the Soviets realized their mistake, they returned to the council and blocked any further measures relative to the Korean

War. Since the United States and its allies were fighting under the
UN banner, Washington wanted further UN authorization for war
measures, including crossing the thirty-eighth parallel to counterattack North Korea. Stymied now by the Soviet veto, the Americans
turned to the General Assembly, securing passage there of a resolution called *Uniting for Peace*. It did not deal with Korea but rather
with the overarching problem of UN paralysis. It provided that,

> if the Security Council, because of lack of unanimity of
> the permanent members, fails to exercise its primary
> responsibility for the maintenance of international
> peace and security in any case where there appears to
> be a threat to the peace, breach of the peace, or act of
> aggression, the General Assembly shall consider the
> matter immediately with a view to making appropriate
> recommendations to Members for collective measures,
> including . . . the use of armed force . . . to restore
> international peace and security.[3]

The Soviet Union, backed by France, protested that this flew in
the face of the charter. Moscow and Paris were right, but Washington had the votes. Based on this arrogated authority, the United
States then succeeded in winning General Assembly endorsement
of its Korea policies. But by the late 1960s, the balance of power
within the General Assembly had shifted, and it was no longer the
United States that had the votes to place security issues before the
General Assembly in this manner. Most often it has been done for
purposes with which Washington is at odds. For example, since
1980 the assembly has held almost continuous "emergency sessions," as they are called, to decry Israel. However, the assembly
has never since Korea gone so far as to authorize the use of force.

Uniting for Peace was the only formal effort ever made to remedy the stillborn status of the charter's structure for enforcing
peace. Beyond the immediate problem of the Korean War, this
effort failed, and, given how regularly it is outvoted in the General Assembly, the United States is fortunate that it did.

Worse still than its failure to act as a barrier to war, in one case the UN actually helped to precipitate conflict. That was the 1967 Six-Day War between Israel and Egypt, Syria, and Jordan. The war issued from a confluence of actions on many sides, including false Soviet intelligence reports, delivered to Arab leaders, of an Israeli mobilization on Syria's border. But the key instigation was a series of belligerent maneuvers by Egypt, including blocking the Straits of Tiran to Israeli shipping, moving several divisions into the Sinai desert near Israel, and numerous warlike declamations.

Yet various retrospectives on the crisis have concluded that Egypt's president, Gamal Abdel Nasser, did not want war with Israel.[4] Nasser was a charismatic revolutionary who aspired to be seen as the leader of the whole Arab world, if not also the Islamic world and Africa. By 1967, he had ruled for fourteen years without much to show for it. He had suffered the humiliation of defeat at Israel's hand in the 1956 Sinai war, and his star had lost some luster. He was also locked in something of a power struggle with Field Marshall Abdul Hakim Amer, chief of the Egyptian military, who seems to have been less reluctant to go to war.

Nasser's goal may have been to pull off some histrionic saber-rattling and perhaps, thereby, to squeeze some concessions out of Israel or the international community and burnish his image as a heroic figure. One of his dramatic gestures was to demand the withdrawal of the UN forces that were stationed in the Sinai and Gaza, all along the border between Egypt and Israel. This United Nations Emergency Force (UNEF) comprised some 4,500 troops manning forty-odd observation posts. It had been created following the 1956 war as part of the deal in which Israel agreed to withdraw from the Sinai, which it had occupied. The UNEF was stationed entirely on the Egyptian side of the border, pursuant to an agreement between Nasser and UN Secretary General Dag Hammarskjöld. It provided that international forces were there at Egypt's sufferance, but that their removal would require consultation with the General Assembly.[5]

Egypt's demand for the removal of UNEF forces was delivered first to their commander, Indar Jit Rikhye, who resisted it, saying that such a request should be addressed to political authorities. The Egyptian ambassador to the UN then met with Secretary General U Thant to demand the withdrawal of UNEF, and this was followed by a letter from the Egyptian foreign minister. Historian Michael Oren has recapitulated the secretary general's reaction:

> [Thant] feared that any attempt to hinder the Egyptian army could endanger the safety of UNEF personnel, and jeopardize future peacekeeping operations elsewhere. Though his own legal counsel firmly advised against taking the "radical action" of bending to Egypt's ultimatum before consulting the relevant UN bodies, U Thant's mind was made up. . . . In a meeting that afternoon with the UNEF Advisory Committee, while Western ambassadors argued strenuously for postponing a final decision, U Thant sided with the Pakistani and Indian delegates in upholding Egypt's right to dismiss the force unilaterally.[6]

By some accounts Nasser himself was caught off-guard by the alacrity with which U Thant obeyed his demand. Dag Hammarskjöld left a memo in which he described having spent seven hours with Nasser in 1957 haggling over the terms for the emplacement of the UNEF. Nasser, he wrote, "very fully understood" that in accepting the text worked out by the two of them, he had agreed to "limiting [Egypt's] freedom of action" with respect to removal of the forces, and that the matter would have to come before the General Assembly.[7] The operative sentence of the letter to U Thant from Egyptian foreign minister Mahmoud Riad read, "I request that the necessary steps be taken for the withdrawal of the force as soon as possible."[8] This wording suggests that the government of Egypt did not expect the hasty withdrawal which, in fact, ensued.

Had the secretary general resisted or delayed, as many around him wanted him to do, it is at least possible that face-saving measures could have been found to avert the conflagration. As it was, UNEF's abrupt withdrawal lit the fuse to the war that burst forth some two weeks later.

In the Middle East, as most everywhere else, the rivalry between the Soviet Union and the United States prevented the UN from functioning as its founders had envisioned. At the same time, the UN contributed little to ameliorating the Cold War. Rather, as the political scientists Anthony Gaglione and Abraham Yeselson pointed out, it became a weapon "employed for the conflict purposes of member states."[9] In jockeying for advantage over its adversary, each side sought to use UN bodies for leverage.

Perhaps more revealing is the fact that when the Cold War ended, the UN played little part in it. The key factor was the rise to power of Mikhail Gorbachev as ruler of the Soviet Union. The Cold War was driven by the Soviets, a logical corollary of the Marxist-Leninist theory that the "socialist camp" was necessarily locked in mortal combat with the forces of world capitalism. Gorbachev jettisoned that theory, and in effect sued for peace. It took several years for the leaders of the West to become satisfied that Gorbachev was sincere, and over this same time the idea itself, which had at first been inchoate, took firmer shape in Gorbachev's mind. The process by which two superpowers liquidated their long, bitter conflict involved many summits and other meetings, and many negotiations and agreements on arms and other issues. What it conspicuously did not involve was any significant peacemaking role on the part of the UN.

With the end of the Cold War in 1989, hopes were kindled that the Security Council, no longer polarized, could begin at last to play the role of peace-enforcer envisioned in the charter. This idea strengthened when the council responded promptly and effectively to Iraq's conquest of Kuwait in 1990, its first post–Cold War test.

But the very next crisis of international peace, which came little more than a year later with the disintegration of Yugoslavia, dashed these hopes. Not only did the Security Council fail to uphold the peace among the elements of what had been Yugoslavia; it actually made things worse. It did this first by adopting a resolution in September 1991 imposing an arms embargo on all parties in Yugoslavia.[10] In theory, this response was evenhanded, but its consequences were unequal, especially as the main bloodletting shifted from Slovenia and Croatia to Bosnia-Herzegovina.

The Serbian aggressors who were out to "cleanse" Bosnia of its plurality Muslim population were scarcely affected by the embargo, since they had at their disposal the formidable arsenal of the Yugoslav army. Their victims, however, were short of weapons, and the embargo contributed to their helplessness.

One might excuse this decision on two grounds. First, the council members wanted to discourage fuel from being added to an internecine fire. Second, they probably did not foresee the perverse effects of their action. But months later, Bosnia-Herzegovina's independence was recognized by most other states, and it was admitted to membership in the UN. This meant that the conflict was no longer internecine, or at least not wholly so, since in addition to Bosnian Serbs, Serbia itself was party to the fighting and to the murderous attacks on civilians. In other words, under well-established principles of international law, this war had become a case of aggression, the very thing which it is the paramount responsibility of the Security Council to prevent or stop.

Moreover, the painfully unequal effects of the embargo had become clear. Seeing this, did the council act to defend Bosnia-Herzegovina? It did not. Did it at least modify its own embargo so that the Bosniacs might defend themselves? On the contrary, it ratified Secretary General Boutros Boutros-Ghali's announced interpretation that the arms embargo, which had been voted against Yugoslavia when it was still a single entity, would apply as well to all of the successor states that devolved from it—aggressor and victim alike.

The wars of Yugoslav disintegration showed that the ineffectiveness of the Security Council as a bulwark of peace was due to causes that lay deeper than the Cold War. The interests of nations differ, and so do their values. The Cold War was an extreme case of this, but even less extreme cases are bound to impede united action. For example, although during the Yugoslav wars the Kremlin was no longer the seat of a Communist government bent on overcoming the capitalist West, it was now the seat of a Russian government pulled by ties of kinship and faith to its fellow Eastern Orthodox Slavs in their conflicts with Muslims, Catholics, and Western Europeans.

The salience of such factors is felt most keenly when the action in question is the use of military force. To rebuke in words a state that misbehaves is one thing; to take up arms against it is quite another. Few nations are prepared to send their sons to die in wars that are fought neither for direct self-defense nor self-aggrandizement, but only to uphold world order. Although the stakes may be real, they are likely to seem too abstract to explain to their own populations. Fewer still have the capability to project force effectively against an aggressor or miscreant far from home. The result, as a 2005 study by the RAND Corporation puts it, is that

> UN operations have almost always been undermanned and under resourced . . . This is not because UN managers believe smaller is better, although some do, but because member states are rarely willing to commit the manpower or the money any prudent military commander would desire.[11]

The failure of the Security Council to establish barriers against breaches of the peace across borders led to a focus on the apparently more modest goal of dampening conflicts within states. This function came to be designated "peacekeeping." In the 1990s, the UN played an effective role in laying to rest conflagrations in Cambodia, East Timor, El Salvador, Namibia, Mozambique, and a few other places. Mostly these were clashes from which the venom had been drawn by the ending of the Cold War. With the world around them no longer polarized, the local parties were ready for compromise, but mutual distrust stood in the way. In such a situation the interposition of a neutral force that could verify to each side that the other was fulfilling the terms of peace was a crucial ingredient. The UN's impartiality was trusted, and it could play this role effectively.

However, in several other situations where one or more of the parties were not ready for peace, the UN's attempts at peacekeeping led to disaster. One such case was Bosnia. After the Security Council's arms embargo had deprived the Bosniacs of the means to defend themselves, it voted in mid-1993 to declare six cities in Bosnia "safe areas," to which Muslims fleeing "ethnic cleansing" might repair.[12] Although the Security Council authorized the use of force in protection of these safe areas, the UN peacekeepers were given rules of engagement that allowed them to fire their weapons only if they themselves were fired upon, not if the people under their putative protection were being shot. Thus, for the better part of a year, under the imperturbable eyes of the UN, Serbian snipers and artillery rained murder and mayhem on Sarajevo and the five other safe areas.

As the war ground on, the top UN officials on the scene—Yasushi Akashi, the secretary general's civilian representative, and generals Michael Rose and Bernard Janvier, successive commanders of the UN peacekeepers—exhibited more sympathy for the Serb aggressors than their Muslim quarry. Rose, for example, once threatened to "carpet-bomb" Bosnian positions, although he always resisted anything more than symbolic strikes against the Serbs; and Janvier deemed it more important to keep his word to Serb commanders than to call in air power to stop the massacre at Srebrenica.[13]

The best construction that can be put on this is that they wanted an end to the conflict at any price, and the shortest path they could see to such an outcome was for the weaker party to surrender. In April 1994, Akashi and Rose gave a press conference at which they denounced America's moral support for the Muslims because it "emboldens [them] to fight on." Then General Rose added, in reference to Muslims living in the towns of Gorazde, Srebrenica, and Zepa, which had been formally declared "safe areas" by the Security Council, "Their only option is to move out or submit to living under Serb rule."[14]

Rose's chilling words were all but an invitation to what transpired a year later, when Serbian forces overran Srebrenica and some five to ten thousand Muslim men were rounded up and exterminated, the worst atrocity in Europe since World War II. The UN did not merely fail to stop or prevent the slaughter at Srebrenica; it helped to bring it about. Rose's irresponsible comments were only the beginning of this complicity.

The UN forces on the ground were called UNPROFOR, an acronym for UN Protection Force, a name which proved bitterly ironic. According to the UN's own subsequent report on the events of Srebrenica, "UNPROFOR commanders . . . convinced the Bosniac commanders that they should sign an agreement in which Bosniac forces would give up their arms to UNPROFOR," in return for various guarantees.[15] Although some said that the exact nature of the guarantees was imprecise, the Bosniacs certainly understood that these meant that the UN Protection Force would protect them. And clearly this was understood by the UN as well.

In July 1995, as Serbian forces pressed in on Srebrenica, Akashi sent a report to the secretariat noting, according to the UN report,

> that the Bosniac Serb commander in Srebrenica had called on UNPROFOR to return the weapons held by it as part of the demilitarization agreement. [Akashi] added that "this is an issue which may well need to be resolved in the near future given the impossibility for [sic] UNPROFOR to defend the safe area."[16]

Some of the military commanders seemed to have a less bleak assessment of the UN's capabilities, but not of its responsibilities. As the report further explained,

> Ramiz Becirovic, acting Commander of Bosniac forces in Srebrenica, asked the UNPROFOR Battalion Commander to give the Bosniacs back the weapons they had surrendered . . . but this request was refused. One of the Dutchbat [acronym for the Dutch battalion that constituted the UNPROFOR force guarding Srebrenica] Commander's superiors, with whom he had consulted on this decision, has since stated that he supported the decision not to hand back the weapons, because "it was UNPROFOR's responsibility to defend the enclave, and not theirs. . . . We didn't want to escalate the situation further by bringing the [Bosnian Serb

Army] and the [army of Bosnia-Herzegovina] into direct fighting."[17]

But UNPROFOR did not defend the enclave. It did not even try to do so except by passive measures such as firing flares at the advancing Serb forces to warn them off and firing some rounds over their heads. For days, as the Serb onslaught intensified, UN commanders debated whether to request an air bombardment by NATO—even as NATO warplanes roamed the skies until they ran out of fuel, waiting for the order to carry out strikes that almost certainly would have stopped the Serbs. But the order never came. Even the UN's own investigation failed to reach a clear conclusion about where in the organization's baroque structure the decision stalled. The report says,

> At least three (but possibly up to five) requests for air support by Dutchbat had been turned down at various levels in the chain of command. Dutchbat had also not fired a single shot directly at the advancing Serb forces.[18]

Some of the UN's dithering involved time-consuming efforts to ascertain the true objectives of the Serbs as they tightened the noose on Srebrenica. Most damningly, the UN's extraordinary inertia may itself have served as a provocation that induced the Serbs to go farther than they had originally intended, energized like sharks sensing blood in the water. The UN's investigation, citing reports unearthed from apparently frustrated members of the UN military mission at the time, offers this stunning confession:

> The report of the United Nations military observers concluded with an assessment that "the BSA [Bosnian Serb Army] offensive may even be widening since the United Nations response has been almost non-existent and the BSA are now in a position to overrun the enclave if they wish." Documents later obtained from Serb sources

appear to suggest that this assessment was correct. Those documents indicate that the Serb attack on Srebrenica initially had limited objectives. Only after having advanced with unexpected ease did the Serbs decide to overrun the entire enclave. Serb civilian and military officials from the Srebrenica area have stated the same thing, adding, in the course of discussions with a United Nations official, that they decided to advance all the way to Srebrenica town when they assessed that UNPROFOR was not willing or able to stop them.[19]

While the debacle of Bosnia was unfolding, other grim events were being played out in Africa. In his final days in office in 1992, President George H. W. Bush had dispatched American forces to Somalia under UN auspices to bring a halt to mass starvation by protecting the delivery of food and medicine. Although Bush's idea was to end the starvation and leave, the Security Council, encouraged by Secretary Boutros-Ghali, set a more ambitious mission, namely the "reestablishment of national and regional institutions and civil administration in the entire country."[20]

Bush's successor, Bill Clinton, agreed reluctantly to Boutros-Ghali's entreaties to leave a substantial number of U.S. troops as the backbone of the UN mission. That mission soon became a target of one of the Somali factions led by Mohamed Farah Aidid; and when twenty-four Pakistani peacekeepers were slaughtered in an ambush by Aidid's men, U.S. forces undertook to suppress that group. In the course of an operation against Aidid's forces in October 1993, two American helicopters were downed, and a company of U.S. Army Rangers was wiped out in the streets of Mogadishu. This precipitated a hasty American departure from Somalia and soon thereafter a termination of the UN mission there.

The toll of the Somalia misadventure was to be counted not only in the lives of Americans and Somalis; it contributed to a more immense tragedy by coloring the international response to events that began to unfold in Rwanda six months later. There, the world's first indisputable case of genocide since the Holocaust unfolded. In the spring of 1994, Hutus slaughtered their Tutsi countrymen (along with moderate Hutus) at a pace that rivaled Hitler's killing of Jews, even without the benefit of the technology of murder that the Nazis devised.

Not only did the UN stand aside as these unspeakable events occurred, but a small UN force that was already on the scene to enforce an earlier peacekeeping agreement was pulled back lest anyone in a blue helmet perish alongside the intended victims. The U.S. government, determined to avoid anything that smacked of a replay of Mogadishu, did more than its share to block any action by the Security Council that could put an American soldier in harm's way. It deliberately understated the tragedy, as the *New York Times* described:

> Trying to avoid the rise of moral pressure to stop the mass killing in Rwanda, the Clinton Administration has instructed its spokesmen not to describe the deaths there as genocide, even though some senior officials believe that is exactly what they represent. . . . American officials say that so stark a label could inflame public calls for action the Administration is unwilling to take. . . . "Genocide is a word that carries an enormous amount of responsibility," a senior Administration official said this week.[21]

Years later, Bill Clinton offered the most grudging of apologies for this. "The international community," he said, "must bear its share of responsibility for this tragedy."[22] He did not bring himself to acknowledge that "the international community" in this instance was first and foremost himself.

If the United States bears much blame for the Rwanda catastrophe, the UN also covered itself in shame. Months before the Rwanda genocide began, General Romeo Dallaire, the Canadian commander of the UN force stationed there since a previous round of violence, had cabled to headquarters with an ominous report. An informant had told him that Hutu extremists were stockpiling weapons and training for a campaign of "extermination."[23] Dallaire proposed to seize the weapons in the hope of disrupting the sanguinary plan. Dallaire's message was received by the UN's Department of Peacekeeping Operations with alarm—not at the prospect of genocide but at the danger that Dallaire might do something risky to prevent it. Clear orders were dispatched, vetoing Dallaire's proposed intervention. "The overriding consideration is the need to avoid entering into a course of action that might lead to the use of force and unanticipated consequences," they read.[24]

When the killing began, Dallaire believed that his forces, augmented by the soldiers that Western governments had sent to evacuate their own nationals, "could easily have stopped the massacres and showed the people at the barriers [that is, the Hutu mobs] that it was dangerous to be there. They would have gone home."[25] But his orders were to the contrary. There was to be no intervention, not even for rescue. As Human Rights Watch reconstructed events,

> Even after the U.N. and the Belgian and French governments had decided that troops under their control would not attempt to restore order in Rwanda, they still had the opportunity to save Rwandan lives in the process of evacuating foreigners. Taking Rwandans out of the country was a solution that could help only a tiny number of those at risk, but the presence of the evacuation force and the convoys they organized presented a chance to bring Rwandans to places of refuge within Kigali. When plans were first discussed for evacuating U.N. personnel, the rule was that no Rwandans, staff or not, could be taken along. Colonel Balis stated that he questioned Dallaire twice about the directive and was told, "Orders from New York: No Locals."[26]

The failures in Bosnia, Somalia, and Rwanda resulted in critical scrutiny of UN peacekeeping operations, including from within the UN itself. Secretary General Boutros-Ghali, who in 1992 had issued a manifesto, *An Agenda for Peace*, that aimed to bring to belated fruition the peace-enforcing role and machinery envisioned in the charter, three years later issued a "Supplement."[27] It acknowledged that in "certain areas . . . unforeseen, or only partly foreseen, difficulties have arisen."[28] The number of governments willing to volunteer troops for perilous UN missions was too few, and the number of troops they offered was too small. Worse, many of those that were offered were of little use. They would arrive, complained Boutros-Ghali, "without the necessary equipment and training."[29] For some strapped governments, that was the whole point: Volunteering soldiers for UN missions was a cost-free way of getting them trained and equipped.

In all of the failed missions, UN peacekeepers had lacked the means, the courage, or the unity to perform effectively. In Bosnia, UNPROFOR lacked the firepower it would have needed to defend the areas it was allegedly protecting, and it also lacked the strength of purpose and unity of command to call in the NATO air support that might have accomplished the job. In Rwanda, writes Michael Barnett, "Bangladeshi peacekeepers even refused to open the gates of the compound to Belgian soldiers who were being chased and cornered by a mob, ostensibly because they believed that the Belgians were marked and thought that the best way to protect themselves was to keep the Belgians outside the compound."[30] In Somalia, the Italian contingent was suspected by other UN elements of secretly abetting the Somali factions with which the UN was locked in deadly combat. American soldiers believed that the Italians were warning the Somalis of impending U.S. raids,[31] and the *Washington Post* reported that Nigerian commanders

> accused the Italian troops of standing by as the Nigerian soldiers—arriving at the check point in open pickup trucks—were being cut down by a torrent of automatic weapons fire. [The] commander of the Nigerian contingent here said of the Italians: "They deliberately left the Nigerians alone. There was no doubt about it." [He] said Italians stationed near the ambush site refused to open fire to assist the Nigerian troops, and at

one point in the firefight even asked the beleaguered Nigerians to move away from an Italian armored vehicle so as not to draw fire to it.[32]

These bitter experiences in the 1990s led to the conclusion that the UN could no more bring a halt to internal conflicts than to international ones. Rather, it could undertake peacekeeping only where all parties to a conflict sought to end it and needed the good offices of a neutral force to reinforce mutual trust or verify the fulfillment of obligations. As Madeleine Albright, who had come to the UN an ardent advocate of "assertive multilateralism," eventually concluded,

> Traditional U.N. peacekeepers lack the mandate, command structure, unity of purpose, and military might to succeed in the more urgent and nasty cases—where the fighting is hot, the innocent are dying, and the combatants oppose an international presence. Such weaknesses, sadly, are inherent in the voluntary and collective nature of the United Nations.[33]

Kofi Annan, who acceded to the post of secretary general from having headed the organization's peacekeeping unit, has said the same: "Peacekeepers must never again be deployed into an environment in which there is no cease-fire or peace agreement."[34] In other words, far from upholding peace internationally or internally against those who would violate it, the best the UN can do is offer a kind of technical assistance in situations in which all the parties want peace. Such assistance can indeed be valuable, but Annan's criterion effectively removes the UN from functions for which it was founded.

What of 1991? Was not the Security Council's authorization of war to restore Kuwait's independence an important exception to this bleak assessment? Yes, it was. But the credit due to the UN for this action must be given with three caveats. First, Saddam Hussein's invasion of Kuwait came at a golden moment of Security Council comity. We were still in the glow of the end of the Cold

War, and the main impetus for Soviet foreign policy at the moment was to be accepted as a "normal" state. Beijing, for its part, was still feeling the pangs of international obloquy over the Tiananmen Square massacre and was in no mood to be defiant.

Second, it is widely acknowledged that the United States blundered badly in not removing Saddam from power at the time it drove his forces from Kuwait. U.S. officials at the time are unanimous in saying that the biggest inhibition to taking such action was that American forces were operating under a UN mandate that would have been exceeded by going after Saddam.

Third, the accomplishments of 1991 were vitiated by the Security Council's unwillingness for many years to enforce the terms of the peace, culminating in 2003.

Nuclear Nonproliferation

There is yet one other function of the UN relative to preserving peace: preventing nuclear proliferation. Following a rueful experience as U.S. permanent representative to the UN in 1975–76, Daniel Patrick Moynihan wrote that the International Atomic Energy Agency "is the one UN institution the world could not very well do without."[35] But while the goal of the IAEA is undoubtedly indispensable, there is ample reason to doubt its effectiveness. Just as UN peacekeeping can work well where the parties all want peace, so the IAEA provides mutual reassurance among states of good faith. Thus, according to John Bolton, then the U.S. undersecretary of state for arms control and international security, the agency spends the majority of its "safeguards" budget monitoring Canada, Japan, and Germany.[36] But for "rogue" regimes, the IAEA has presented few barriers.

Consider the case of Iraq. It was an original signer of the Non-Proliferation Treaty (NPT) in 1968, becoming a member when the treaty came into force in 1970. Accordingly, Iraq entered into a "safeguards" agreement with the IAEA, declared its nuclear facilities, and submitted to periodic examination of these by IAEA inspectors.

Inspections continued through the 1980s, right up until Iraq's invasion of Kuwait in 1990. At that time, Jon Jennekens, the deputy
director of the agency and the head of its Safeguards Division, told
journalists that Iraq's cooperation with the IAEA inspectors had
been "exemplary." The responsible Iraqi officials, he said "have
made every effort to demonstrate that Iraq is a solid citizen" in its
compliance with the nonproliferation system.[37]

It turned out, however, that all of the ingratiating cooperation
had been a smokescreen. Saddam Hussein's regime had been working almost from the start to develop a nuclear weapon. Using its
declared goal of peaceful nuclear energy as a cover under which to
import components and enable its scientists and technicians to
accumulate know-how, the Iraqi regime developed "an elaborate
strategy . . . to deceive and manipulate the agency," explained
Khidir Hamza, a leading Iraqi nuclear scientist who defected to the
United States in 1994.[38]

The deception, which according to Hamza began in 1974, succeeded for seventeen years, until Iraq was defeated in the first Gulf
War. Then much of it (though not the whole) was laid bare, including some piquant details. One such was described by arms-control
expert Gary Milhollin:

> Before a shocked group of inspectors, a senior Iraqi
> official calmly revealed that Iraq had . . . extract[ed]
> plutonium in violation of Iraqi promises to the I.A.E.A.
> To make matters worse, the Iraqi official was himself
> a former I.A.E.A. inspector. He told his outraged ex-
> colleagues that his I.A.E.A. experience had made it eas-
> ier to dupe them.[39]

The essence of the Iraqi deception was simple, and it pointed to
a basic flaw in the nonproliferation regime overseen by the IAEA:
The inspectors inspect the sites that the subject-nation declares, but
they have little authority or practical means for discovering unde-
clared sites. A state intent on cheating offers up its nonmilitary sites
for inspection and conceals the location of its weapons program.

Opinions of Western experts vary as to how close Iraq came to having "the bomb" at the time its invasion of Kuwait provoked the American-led counterattack. David Kay, who headed the IAEA inspections of Iraq following the 1991 Gulf War, testified that he discovered that Iraq had been within twelve to eighteen months of acquiring enough fissile material to produce a weapon.[40] The Federation of American Scientists reports, "Several experts familiar with the inspections believe that Iraq could . . . probably have produced a workable device in as little as 6 to 24 months, had they decided to seize foreign-supplied HEU [highly enriched uranium] from under safeguards." Even relying on domestic fuel, the program might have unfolded in a similar time frame, according to the report:

> Iraq had a very well-funded nuclear weapons program aimed at the indigenous development and exploitation of technologies for the production of weapon-usable nuclear material and the development and production of nuclear weapons, with a target date of 1991 for the first weapon. It is reasonable to suppose that the first device, containing indigenously produced HEU, would not have been available before late 1992.[41]

When the veil was torn off the Iraqi programs by the American conquest, Hans Blix, then the agency's director, confessed that the IAEA had been "fooled" by Baghdad.[42] He explained further:

> The question is often asked whether there is any way in which through inspection we can be certain of obtaining knowledge about every gram of enriched uranium or about every relevant piece of nuclear equipment in a country. The answer to this question, whether in the case of Iraq or any other country, is negative. It is not possible for an international inspectorate to go to every building and basement in a country in search of nuclear relevant objects and material.[43]

Blix's acknowledgment, however, contained a straw man. The question is not whether a gram of enriched uranium could go undetected, but whether many grams could, and be enough to build a weapon; indeed, whether entire nuclear facilities could be successfully hidden. And the short answer is yes.

The same tactics that Iraq used have also been used by Iran, which also has been a party to the Non-Proliferation Treaty since 1970. In 1992, the Iranian People's Mojahedin, an opposition group, identified two sites in Iran that it said were being used for the clandestine development of nuclear weapons, and news leaks from sources within the U.S. government lent weight to suspicions that such a program was underway. In response to the allegations, the IAEA arranged with the Iranian government to send a team of inspectors to visit six or seven sites in Iran.

After several days of inspections, the team leader, Jon Jennekens, the same senior IAEA official who affirmed Iraq's cooperation, declared that "at sites that we visited we were able to conclude that the activities being carried out there were entirely in accord with the declared purpose of the facilities."[44] And he added, "We are pleased to confirm that there does not seem to be a shred of evidence on the allegations that were made in the media. Nothing we have seen proves that there is any activity here against the peaceful principles of nuclear policy."[45]

Despite some caveats in an IAEA press release about the limitations of the team's observations, this was widely taken as a clean bill of health for Teheran on the nuclear question. Reportedly, the American member of the agency's board of governors protested that the exercise had been "naïve," a characterization that earned a rebuke from IAEA director Blix.[46] Despite the findings of this mission, within less than a year news reports said that the CIA had concluded Iran was well along in a drive to develop such weapons, and estimated that it might achieve this goal by the year 2000.[47]

A decade later, in 2002, fresh accusations were announced by the People's Mojahedin, this time of clandestine Iranian nuclear programs in two previously unknown locations, the towns of Natranz and Arak. This precipitated new inquiries by the IAEA, and this time Iran, with little way out, acknowledged that it had been furnishing the IAEA with misleading information for eighteen years. It continued to claim, implausibly, that its concealed nuclear activities were designed only for the generation of energy. Far from suffering penalties for this long history of misbehavior, Iran was congratulated for having belatedly come clean.

But it had not come clean. Rather, Teheran seems to have confessed as little as it felt it could get away with while continuing its deception. A year later, in September 2003, a resolution of the IAEA board of governors reflected the agency's mounting frustration. The measure expressed

> grave concern that, more than one year after initial IAEA inquiries to Iran about undeclared activities, Iran has still not enabled the IAEA to provide the assurances required by Member States that all nuclear material in Iran is declared and submitted to Agency safeguard and that there are no undeclared nuclear activities in Iran.

It complained that "information and access were at times slow in coming and incremental, that some of the information was in contrast to that previously provided by Iran." And it called upon Iran "to ensure that there are no further failures to report material, facilities and activities that Iran is obliged to report pursuant to its safeguards agreement."[48]

That resolution demanded Iran's full compliance by the end of October, and just before that deadline Iran submitted a new declaration about its nuclear programs couched in conciliatory terms. In response, the board declared that it "welcomes Iran's offer of active cooperation and openness and its positive response" while warning Teheran that "the Board considers it essential that the declarations that have now been made by Iran amount to the correct, complete and final picture of Iran's past and present nuclear programme."[49]

But four months later, the agency was recognizing that it had received nothing of the sort. At its March 2004 meeting, the board registered its serious concern that the declarations made by Iran in October 2003 did not amount to the complete and final picture of Iran's past and present nuclear program considered essential by the Board's November 2003 resolution, in that the Agency has since uncovered a number of omissions—e.g., a more advanced centrifuge design than previously declared, including associated research, manufacturing and testing activities; two mass spectrometers used in the laser enrichment program; and designs for the construction of hot cells at the Arak heavy water research reactor—which require further investigation, not least as they may point to nuclear activities not so far acknowledged by Iran.[50]

And a year after that, Iran was still prevaricating, and the IAEA was still issuing sonorous warnings. Its ultimate sanction is to refer a country to the Security Council. The U.S. government had been pressing for some time for such a referral. But this was resisted by America's European allies, who labored to bring Iran around through incentives and friendly negotiations. Gradually, Teheran's recalcitrance drove the Europeans closer to Washington's position.

But even if the matter is referred to the Security Council, so what? Russia and China may protect Iran with their vetoes, or fellow members of the Non-Aligned Movement, the UN's largest bloc, could protect it with their votes. Even America's allies might not go for any measures tough enough to make Teheran change its ways. A "British official" told the *New York Times*, as the European negotiations with Iran seemed to reach a dead end, that Security Council

> sanctions could take various calibrated forms, including a simple condemnation but moving on to a formal prohibition on uranium enrichment. . . . There could also be individual sanctions on nuclear industry officials or broader sanctions that might affect Iran's economy. But

before reaching that stage, other British officials said, Britain wants a broad international consensus for action against Iran if the negotiations . . . fail.[51]

In other words, referral to the Security Council, the supreme threat that the IAEA has held over Iran ever since the 2002 revelations, is hollow. The Security Council is unlikely to authorize force or even a complete embargo. (In light of its unhappy experience with the embargo of Iraqi oil, which seemed to penalize innocent civilians more than the miscreant government and led to the largest scandal in UN history, is there any chance it would now embargo Iranian oil?) Whatever penalties it might exact are unlikely to deter Iran from its nuclear quest, any more than the League of Nations' half-hearted embargo on Italy deterred it from the conquest of Abyssinia (Ethiopia) in 1935. In the meantime, Israeli and American governments and Iranian dissidents all continue to claim they have evidence that Iran has still other nuclear weapons development programs it has never revealed.

As in the case of Iraq, the IAEA was unable to block Iran's nuclear progress, and in some unintended ways it might even have boosted Iran's weapons program. Henry Sokolski, a former Defense Department nonproliferation official, said that Teheran

> requested to have Iranian nuclear inspectors gain free access to all of Japan's nuclear reprocessing facilities— the same facilities that the Iranians are suspected of trying to build on their own soil to produce weapons plutonium. It also has taken full advantage of IAEA scholarship funding to help train Iranian technicians in sensitive nuclear fuel cycle technology. Because of its good standing with the IAEA, Iran has managed to get the agency to plead Iran's case to Germany to finish the two nearly complete pressurized water reactors. The most important benefit of Iran's participation in the IAEA, though, has been the legitimacy it has lent to Iran's nuclear activities.[52]

Another lawless state, North Korea, used a different strategy in developing its nuclear arsenal, which is believed to comprise anywhere from two to seven or more bombs. It signed the Non-Proliferation Treaty in 1985 and then dragged out for seven years the required inspection plan with the IAEA that is supposed to be agreed upon within eighteen months after a state signs the NPT. Even then, its list of sites subject to inspection omitted facilities that seemed obviously part of its nuclear program. When the IAEA protested the omissions, Pyongyang announced it would withdraw from the treaty. Then, it "suspended" its withdrawal in return for some incentives from the United States. The to-ing and fro-ing continued until 1994, when the United States and North Korea reached a showdown. By that time, according to news reports, the CIA had concluded that North Korea already possessed one or two nuclear weapons. In all likelihood, these were produced during the eight years after Pyongyang signed the NPT, while it was dancing around the IAEA.

The 1991 revelations of Iraqi deception spurred efforts to strengthen the IAEA. In 1997 the agency unveiled its model "Additional Protocol." States that were party to the Non-Proliferation Treaty were henceforth encouraged to supplement their safeguards agreement with such a protocol. It would furnish the IAEA with more information about nuclear capabilities than had been required by the traditional safeguards agreement, and it would facilitate wider inspections. While this was a step forward, it was a limited one. Nuclear expert Theodore Hirsch summarized it:

> The Additional Protocol . . . can be characterized as an effort to transform IAEA inspectors from accountants to detectives. But exactly what investigative powers does the Additional Protocol bestow? Does it provide for surprise inspections anytime, anywhere? Does it provide for more intrusive inspections? Does it allow for challenge inspections based on other states' allegations? In fact, while providing a significant enhancement of the IAEA's inspection mandate, it does not of these things.

> The Additional Protocol is best understood not as a
> panacea, but as a powerful, albeit limited, tool for deter-
> ring noncompliance with the NPT. It does not eliminate
> the possibility of secret nuclear weapons development,
> but it makes pursuing such a program more costly and
> greatly increases the odds of being caught.[53]

Whatever benefits the Additional Protocol may offer, however, are dependent on two key conditions: that critical states will sign it, and that the IAEA officers and governors will use diligently whatever new leverage it affords. There is no reason for optimism on either score. When the model Optional Protocol was released, the first three states to sign it and bring it into force were Australia, Jordan, and the Holy See—not ones that have been causing many sleepless nights. Of the worrisome regimes, only Iran and Libya have signed the protocol, but as of the summer of 2005 neither had yet legally brought it into force. As for the willingness of the IAEA and its member states to wield this new tool with rigor against potential violators, the fact is that even under the old safeguards system, the IAEA had much the same power, through the proce- dure called "special inspections," but it was unwilling to use it for fear of ruffling feathers.

In sum, there is little assurance that the innovation of the Addi- tional Protocol will provide a comforting answer to the disquieting question raised by the cases of Iraq, Iran, and North Korea: Is the IAEA a real barrier against the acquisition of nuclear weapons by the world's most irresponsible regimes, or is it merely a kind of Maginot line that generates only a false sense of security?

A Moral Beacon?

If, as Madeleine Albright's experience led her to conclude ruefully, the very "nature of the UN" rendered it impotent to fulfill the ambitious function of peace maintenance for which it was created, the organization still might have been able to play an extremely beneficial role in world affairs as a kind of moral beacon. Even while weak in material power, the UN could nonetheless have been highly influential had its practices remained faithful to the lofty humanitarian impulses articulated in the charter. But, alas, the UN's record is quite to the contrary.

First, there is the moral tone of the institution itself. Far from reflecting the uplift of its noble purposes, the organization's bureaucracy, some eighteen thousand strong, is notorious for lethargy and featherbedding. As Dick Thornburgh reported to Boutros-Ghali at the conclusion of his tenure as undersecretary general for administration and management, "Nearly everyone of my senior management colleagues in the Secretariat and many staff members as well have complained about the 'deadwood' problem."[54]

The level of salaries for professional staff is determined on the basis of the "Noblemaire Principle," according to which, as the UN's website explains, "the international civil service should be able to recruit staff from its Member States, including the highest-paid. Therefore, the salaries of Professional staff are set by reference to the highest-paying national civil service."[55] Undersecretaries general are currently paid $250,000 per year—in other words, 40 percent more than a member of the U.S. cabinet. And there are so many of these "USGs" that the undersecretary general for management recently noted, "It is not possible for all USGs to report to the Secretary-General."[56]

UN salaries are high by American standards, and they are considerably higher by the standards of developing countries from which most UN employees come. They are garnished with generous "perks," which include housing allowances, private-school tuition for their children, hospitality funds, and more, all of it free from taxes in the countries where they work. They also enjoy diplomatic immunity which shields them from punishment for petty crimes. (For more serious offenses, the UN will lift their immunity.)

These positions are therefore plums, which generates an impetus to create more of them. Since the wealthiest fourteen member-states (the so-called Geneva group) provide 80 percent of the UN's income, there is little incentive for the other 177 members to hold down costs. Boutros-Ghali remarked in a moment of candor that "the third world is for proliferation [of UN offices], all because of the possibilities of jobs or for prestige. Poor countries want five offices, not one, because all the nieces and daughters of the President work as secretaries."[57]

The problem is not merely the impetus for featherbedding, but also the demand by member-states for their share of the UN pie. Therefore, positions are filled not on the basis of skills and qualifications, but by nationality. As international legal scholar Ruth Wedgwood describes it,

> Under the General Assembly's dictated personnel rules, the UN Secretariat cannot consider candidates for permanent positions unless they are nationals of currently "underrepresented" countries . . . The stated justification for this limited talent search is Article 101 of the UN Charter, which says that "due regard shall be paid to the importance of recruiting the staff on as wide a geographical basis as possible." But the General Assembly has acted to make this a *de facto* sinecure system. Many countries are tempted to "colonize" the secretariat, making sure they get their soft guarantee of at least 6 positions . . . because it is widely believed that it pays to have a friend inside the system to influence decisions.[58]

Although Article 100 of the UN charter stipulates that employees are to function as servants of the world body, uninfluenced by their home countries, this provision is ignored quite cynically, with staff being instructed and sometimes even recalled by their own governments. Some also receive pay supplements, while others have to turn their pay over to their regimes. Such practices occur not only with the organization's professional staff, but also with soldiers on peacekeeping missions, many of whom come from poor countries. The peacekeepers are assigned an international rate of pay, but in many cases their governments keep these stipends and pay the troops only their regular military salaries, pocketing the difference. Lamely, the High-Level Panel on Threats, Challenges, and Change appealed to member-states to "recommit themselves to Articles 100 and 101," the latter of which states that "the paramount consideration" in staffing the UN should be "securing the highest standards of efficiency, competence, and integrity."[59]

Equally cynical, vote-trading is a familiar practice, resulting in such anomalies as the election of Libya to chair the 2002 session of the Commission on Human Rights. It has been quipped that Africa is speckled with soccer stadiums built with Chinese yuan in exchange for votes to shield Beijing from human rights criticism.

Such deals are scarcely limited to poor countries. After France refused to join America in backing a resolution to put China on the agenda of the Commission on Human Rights in 1997, Beijing announced during a visit by French president Jacques Chirac that it was placing a $1.5 billion order with Airbus Industries in place of its previous supplier, Boeing. Instead of supporting criticism of China by the commission, Chirac announced a "new approach," which, as explained by Agence France-Presse, "gives more emphasis to different political traditions and gave more importance to 'dialogue over confrontation.'"[60]

"On the subject of . . . human rights," enthused Chinese president Jiang Zemin, "France has made a wise decision."[61] In particular, Jiang's and Chirac's joint declaration said: "China expresses its appreciation for the constructive attitude taken by France in the framework of the United Nations Commission on Human Rights."[62] A few years later, when China and France colluded to block America from being elected to the commission, the *New York Times* reported that, according to the French UN ambassador, "approaching human-rights issues with cooperation and dialogue rather than confrontation . . . worked well with China."[63] So, apparently, it did—but not for the benefit of human rights.

In a similar vein, when an incompetent Japanese chief of the World Health Organization (WHO) was challenged for reelection in 1992, Rosemary Righter recounted that Tokyo

> invited . . . board members to Japan shortly before the
> vote and, according to U.S. State Department officials,
> had threatened to cut its imports from two countries
> with board representation and made known to others
> that Japanese aid to their country happened currently to
> be under review.[64]

In addition, a British government investigation discovered that a
Japanese underling of the incumbent had circumvented WHO procedures in awarding five contracts of up to $150,000 to entities in
which various members of the WHO board had interests.[65]

UN peacekeepers and aid workers have been accused of improprieties on numerous occasions, perhaps because they are dispatched into lawless areas and are not themselves subject to clear
authority. In 2001, a report by the High Commissioner for Refugees
and the Save the Children Fund alleged that UN personnel in
Guinea, Liberia, and Sierra Leone had "used the positions to elicit
sexual favors from children, primarily adolescent girls."[66]

In 2004, similar reports about the UN peacekeeping operation
in the Congo prompted an inquiry by the UN's Office of Internal
Oversight Services (OIOS) into "allegations of sexual exploitation
and abuse of local . . . women and girls." Although its investigation
"was hampered by problems in obtaining the requisite assistance
and cooperation from two military contingents," as it reported,
OIOS was able to satisfy itself that the charges were true. Its report
concluded that "the problem was serious and ongoing. Equally dis-
turbing was the lack of a protection and deterrence program, even
at the present time."[67]

Further, reports of financial irregularities have swirled around
UN war crimes tribunals. An investigation of the tribunal established to punish those responsible for the Rwanda genocide led
to the dismissal of the tribunal's chief administrative officer and
the deputy prosecutor. OIOS also found that defense attorneys for
the Serb officials being tried in The Hague for war crimes in
Bosnia allegedly kicked back part of their UN-paid fees to
the defendants.[68]

OIOS had been created in the mid-1990s in response to wide-spread suspicions that the insular nature of the UN served to shield misbehavior by UN staff. The U.S. government exerted what Madeleine Albright called "enormous diplomatic effort" to secure the creation of OIOS to serve as an internal watchdog.[69] Secretary General Boutros-Ghali boasted that the new office would "carry out increased inspections, with full independence and without interference."[70] But a recent lurid case reveals how far this is from the reality.

In April 2004, an employee of the UN High Commissioner for Refugees (UNHCR) filed a sexual harassment complaint against the high commissioner, former Netherlands prime minister Ruud Lubbers. She said that in December he had touched her demonstratively and inappropriately in front of two of his male deputies as she was leaving a meeting. The allegation was investigated promptly by OIOS, with the assistance of UNHCR's own Office of the Inspector General.

By June the inquiry was complete. The investigators found that the evidence sustained the allegation. Lubbers denied the story, as did the two deputies. But the three men's versions were incompatible. One deputy denied that any physical contact had occurred, while the other said Lubbers had touched the woman in a way that was "overly familiar," but not exactly as the complainant had claimed. Lubbers initially denied he had touched the woman at all, but when confronted with the second deputy's account, he admitted having touched her, while denying any impropriety and describing himself as a "physical" and "friendly" person. In contrast, the investigators found the woman's credibility to be strong. They interviewed several people to whom she had brought her story, "either immediately or shortly after the incident," and found that "she had spoken with them in detail and with consistency."[71]

Moreover, in the course of its inquiry, OIOS investigators were told by various UNHCR staff members of other women who had confided about similar behavior on the part of Lubbers. They found four—two members of the staff and two who worked closely with UNHCR while employed by allied agencies—who were willing to tell their stories. In all four cases, the investigators found witnesses to whom the women had related the incidents at the time they happened.[72]

To top this off, OIOS found that Lubbers "extensively and intentionally abused his authority as High Commissioner in his intense, pervasive and intimidating attempts to influence the outcome of the investigation."[73] He inappropriately discussed the complaint with potential witnesses and, said OIOS, "may well have influenced the statements of at least two subordinates."[74] He tasked his own inspector general's office "to ascertain who was cooperating with OIOS" and with whom the complainant had consulted.[75] He circulated a note to all UNHCR staff aiming to impeach the credibility of the complainant as well as another female staff member whom he apparently feared might bring similar charges.[76] And other staff members "told OIOS investigators that they were afraid to discuss the case for fear of retaliation."[77]

In conclusion, OIOS found that Lubbers "lack[ed] the requisite integrity" for his job and recommended that "appropriate action be taken." Secretary General Kofi Annan received this report, which he kept secret (it still is secret, but a copy fell into my hands) and summarily overruled it. "I find that the complaint against Mr. Lubbers cannot be sustained," he declared, although he made no claim to have any new facts that were unavailable to the investigators, nor did he explain any way in which he faulted their findings or reasoning.[78]

So much for independent oversight; and there the matter would have rested, except for the coincidence of revelations of misconduct in the UN's oil-for-food program. Just months after he had peremptorily dismissed the case against Lubbers, Annan found himself fighting to preserve his own reputation against the taint of a scandal in which the name of his son and an important aide figured prominently. Suddenly, in mid-February, he saw the UNHCR case in a new light, called Lubbers in, and told him he would have to resign. Lubbers yielded, firing off an angry letter complaining that "despite all my loyalty, insult has been added to injury."[79] Annan's spokesmen put it about that he had been unable to act against Lubbers earlier because the legal grounds were weak, but they did not explain what had changed in the intervening six months to enable the secretary general to reverse himself.

As an almost comic footnote to this sorry story, the head of OIOS was himself accused of sexual improprieties in mid-April, 2004, and Annan also dismissed those charges, leading to a vote of "no confidence" in him on the part of the union representing UN employees.[80] Nor was this the end of ironies. Having reduced OIOS to impotence by dismissing out-of-hand its finding against Lubbers, Annan proposed in his March 2005 omnibus UN reform plan that "the General Assembly commission a comprehensive review of the Office of Internal Oversight Services with view to strengthening its independence and authority as well as its expertise and capacity."[81]

Buffeted by criticism from without and within, Annan ordered an opinion survey to be conducted among UN employees about their views of the institution's integrity. An arcane matrix of questions formulated by the outside consultants who ran the survey were grouped into three broad categories. Employees registered a total score of seventy-four out of a possible one hundred in rating their job satisfaction. But they gave a score of only fifty-two on the questions that assessed the institution's "integrity," and a score of forty-nine on those that reflected their level of "trust" in the institution.[82]

Whatever corruption might have tainted the UN over the years paled in comparison to the scandal that rocked the institution in 2004 over its "oil-for-food" program with Iraq. It may turn out to be, in dollar terms, the largest financial scandal in history. This program had been initiated in 1996 pursuant to a resolution passed the year before by the Security Council at the suggestion of UN officials. It was designed to alleviate the suffering of Iraqi civilians caused by the ongoing economic embargo that had been imposed by the Security Council on Iraq when that country invaded Kuwait in 1990. Under the terms of the 1995 resolution, Iraq was allowed to export specified quantities of oil and to use the proceeds to import civilian goods, with all of the transactions supervised by the UN. The ouster of the Iraqi government in 2003 by U.S. and allied invaders led to the discovery of Iraqi government documents revealing that the UN overseers had failed to prevent the regime from turning the program to its own purposes. Among many abuses, the documents revealed a far-reaching campaign of bribery designed to improve Iraq's international standing. Among those listed as having received bribes in the form of negotiable vouchers to purchase Iraq oil at a discount were British, French, and Russian politicians, the Popular Front for the Liberation of Palestine, and Benon Sevan, the executive director of the oil-for-food program itself.[83]

Sevan's role severely increased the embarrassment this episode caused the UN. Sevan, a Cypriot who had spent forty years on the staff of the UN, had worked his way up to the position of undersecretary general. When the oil-for-food program was created, he was appointed by Kofi Annan to be its executive director. It was bad enough that the program had generated an immense slush fund to finance the nefarious activities of the Saddam regime. It was worse that the highest UN official involved with the program apparently used it to enrich himself.

Faced with these explosive allegations and indignation over his initially low-key response to them, Secretary-General Annan appointed the Independent Inquiry Committee into the United Nations Oil-for-Food Programme, the so-called Volcker Commission. Its report showed that Sevan not only had accepted emoluments from the Iraqi regime; he had taken the initiative in soliciting them.[84]

In reconstructing events, the inquiry found that within about eight months of his appointment, Sevan began suggesting to Iraqi officials in New York and Baghdad that they might allocate some oil sales to a company he knew. His interest, he said, was to "help a friend."[85] Iraqi officials complied and assigned 1.8 million barrels to the firm Sevan mentioned, African Middle East Petroleum (AMEP). Over the next few years, AMEP received a total of 7.3 million barrels. It did not, however, take physical possession of the oil. Rather, it turned around and sold its allocations at once to other companies for a price higher than it had paid. Through these paper transactions it cleared some $1.5 million, according to the figures put together by the Volcker Commission.[86]

Over this same period, Sevan began to list substantial sums of cash income on his annual financial disclosure forms as a UN official. He claimed to have received this cash, $160,000 over four years, from his aunt. But the Volcker Commission found this explanation implausible. The aunt was living on a small Cypriot government pension in a two-room apartment in Cyprus, and no one who knew her believed that she had any such money to spare.[87]

Moreover, Sevan's credibility with the committee was low, as the investigators caught him in a pattern of deception regarding his connection with AMEP. Whereas he began by claiming he had only met the company's owner, Fakery Abdelnour, on one occasion, he gradually acknowledged, when confronted with phone records and other evidence that contradicted his original version, that their relationship was much more than that. "I came to like the guy," Sevan explained. "He is an interesting character."[88] Also, although Sevan claimed that he had not asked Iraqi officials to allocate any oil to AMEP, he later allowed that he "might have mentioned" the company to the Iraqi oil minister, Amer Muhammed Rashid.[89]

The taint of scandal brushed close to the secretary general as well, in the form of questions about the activities of his son, Kojo Annan, and his own knowledge of them. When Kojo graduated from college in 1995, his father had a conversation with Michael Wilson, an old family friend who was an executive of the Cotecna Company, about the possible employment of Kojo by that firm.[90] Four years before that, Cotecna had written to Kofi Annan, then the UN's controller, seeking a contract in connection with the oil-for-food program, which was only in the planning stages. Nothing came of this letter at the time because the program did not come into being for several more years. Cotecna's specialty was the inspection of goods for shipment. After several weeks of training, twenty-two-year-old Kojo was taken on by Cotecna as a junior liaison officer. The Volcker Commission makes clear that young Kojo's chief asset to the firm was "his perceived business connections and standing," which is apparently a euphemism for his genealogy, since there is no suggestion that he had any prior business experience.[91]

Two years later, Kojo ceased to be a regular employee of the firm but continued to be paid by it as a consultant. According to the Volcker Commission, "Mr. Wilson of Cotecna faxed a letter . . . indicating that Kojo Annan had resigned his consultancy on October 9, 1998 . . . in order to avoid a conflict of interest."[92] The significance of the date is that this was the day on which the UN issued the "request for proposals" that resulted in the contract for Cotecna to inspect shipments under the oil-for-food program. The resignation, however, was simply a smokescreen. In lieu of the consulting arrangement, Cotecna began at once to pay Kojo a monthly fee of $2,500 in return for a promise not to offer his services to any of Cotecna's competitors. Such "no-compete" agreements are not unusual, but it is not clear that Kojo Annan had any knowledge or talents to offer other than his status as the son of the secretary general.

Moreover, the "resignation" was quickly ignored. The investigators discovered that "Cotecna continued to make consulting fee payments to Kojo Annan above and beyond the stipulated . . . noncompetition payment." It also continued to pay the charges he ran up on a company credit card, and for his airfare on several trips between Europe and Africa.[93]

Both Cotecna and Kojo worked assiduously to cover their financial arrangement. The payments continued into 2004, the Volcker Commission discovered, although the parties had claimed that the arrangement had terminated years before. For a large part of the time, the payments were made from the accounts of two other firms owned by Robert and Elie Massey, the owners of Cotecna. And for several years the funds were paid into the Swiss bank account of a dummy firm, Westexim, registered by a friend of Kojo's. Bank records show that the deposits into Westexim were followed on a monthly basis by automatic transfers into Kojo's personal bank account.[94]

The Volcker Commission found Kojo's "inability to explain the secretive manner of his continued financial dealings with Cotecna" to be "problematic," and it said that other things he had asserted were "difficult to accept."[95] After much prodding by the commission to reveal his financial records, Kojo produced the statements from a single bank account showing payments from Cotecna, or "possibly" from Cotecna, amounting to $582,603.[96] The commission noted that this omitted entirely any records from any other accounts he might hold, notably including those of a company called Sutton Investments Ltd. that Kojo had created expressly to do subcontracting for Cotecna.[97] When the commission persisted in its inquiries into Kojo's finances, he ceased to cooperate.[98]

For their part, Cotecna's owners lied outright to the commission, claiming at first that the firm's payments to Kojo ended in 1998. When confronted with evidence to the contrary, Robert Massey claimed he had simply forgotten about his ongoing financial arrangement with Kojo, since the payments were automatic, but this, too, turned out to be a lie. Each of the payments—and since they were at least monthly for more than five years there must have been scores of them—had to be individually requisitioned and signed for, and a large number had been signed for by none other than Robert Massey.[99]

As for Kofi Annan's role in all of this, the Volcker investigation found no evidence that "the selection of Cotecna in 1998 was subject to any affirmative or improper influence of the Secretary-General in the bidding or selection process."[100] And this prompted Kofi to say that he had been "vindicated." But the commission did question his behavior on two points. First, it reported that he had told the commission (as his spokesmen had claimed publicly) that he had had no contact with Cotecna before it won the oil-for-food contract. But when, in a search of the files contained on the computer of the secretary general's assistant, two appointments with Elie Massey were discovered, he revised his account to acknowledge two meetings with Massey in the two years before the contract was awarded. One had been arranged by Kojo.[101]

The second point on which the commission chastised Annan was his handling of a story that appeared in the *Sunday Telegraph* (London) in January 1999, reporting that a firm that employed the son of the secretary general had recently secured a UN contract.[102] Annan asked his *chef de cabinet*, Iqbal Riza, to look into the matter, and Riza passed the question down to a subordinate, who reported back within a day in the form of two memos. One asserted that "recent discussions with [the two UN procurement officials involved in awarding the contract] confirm that they were not aware of, and, therefore, could not be influenced by, Mr. Kojo Annan's affiliation with Cotecna." The other reported, "It has been brought to my attention that Mr. Kojo Annan resigned from Cotecna on 9 October 1998."

With these reassurances, the matter was closed as far as the secretary general was concerned. The Volcker Commission found that this "inquiry initiated by the Secretary-General was inadequate, and the Secretary-General should have referred the matter to an appropriate United Nations Department (Office of Internal Oversight Services and/or Office of Legal Affairs) for a thorough and independent investigation."[103]

Even with these criticisms, the Volcker report prompted the resignation of two of the commission's own investigators, former FBI officer Robert Parton and Miranda Duncan, who reportedly believed that the Volcker Commission had shielded the secretary general from the full censure due him.[104]

The venality and corruptibility of various UN officials and national politicians touched by Iraqi oil, while sensational, was only the capstone on the larger scandal. According to Charles Duelfer, the U.S. official charged with making sense of Iraq's weapons program, some twenty-one billion dollars in kickbacks were skimmed from the UN-administered oil transactions, including funds that may have gone for weapons and terrorism, and to line the pockets of UN officials. Duelfer notes that after the oil-for-food program began at the end of 1996, and funds began to flow into Iraqi government coffers, "The budget of [Iraq's] Military Industrial Commission (MIC) surged from $7.8 million in 1998 to $350 million in 2001. In 2003 Iraq had budgeted $500 million for MIC."[105]

Responsibility for oversight of the program lay ambiguously with both the Security Council and the UN secretariat. In practice, as Claudia Rossett, the journalist who has followed the story most closely, points out, only the United States and Britain among the Security Council members wanted to keep a sharp eye on the program, but their concern focused on preventing militarily usable goods from reaching Saddam under its aegis, not on larger issues of corruption. The other key Security Council members would have reduced or eliminated the existing sanctions on Saddam's regime, had they had their way. Thus, they had little desire to monitor the program strictly, and what desire they had was vitiated further by their various political and financial ties to Iraq.

The secretariat, which administered the program with a staff of nearly five thousand employees, was better equipped to oversee it, but shrouded its activities in secrecy. Rossett points out that the oil-for-food office

> released long lists representing billions of dollars in business but noting only the date, country of origin, whether or not the contract had been approved for release of funding, and highly generic descriptions of goods. Typical of the level of detail were notations like "electric motor" from France, "adult milk" from Saudi Arabia, "detergent" from Russia, "cable" from China.[106]

UN spokesmen have pointed out that the program was often audited. And so it was: The Office of Internal Oversight Services produced some fifty-five audits. But these were shared only with the UN secretariat, not with the member-states, and certainly not with the public. Until scandal broke, the audits remained secret.

After a time, it was agreed to alleviate some of the confusion in oversight authority by leaving the supervision of "humanitarian" goods entirely in the hands of the secretariat. "The next month," according to Rossett, "'humanitarian' became a broad category indeed":

> On June 2, Annan approved a newly expanded shopping list by Saddam that the Secretariat dubbed "Oil-for-Food Plus." This added ten new sectors to be funded by

the program, including "labor and social affairs," "information," "justice," and "sports." Either the Secretary-
General had failed to notice or he did not care that none
of these had anything to do with the equitable distribution of relief. By contrast, they had everything to do with
the running of Saddam's totalitarian state. "Labor,"
"information," and "justice" were the realms of Baathist
party patronage, propaganda, censorship, secret police,
rape rooms, and mass graves. As for sports, that was the
favorite arena of Saddam's sadistic son Uday, already
infamous for torturing Iraqi athletes.[107]

It is easy to understand why UN officials—or anyone else—would
have wanted to alleviate the suffering of Iraqi civilians caused by
the sanctions aimed at Saddam. But why would they want to have
alleviated the debilities placed on the regime? That the UN authorized transactions in these areas was itself a scandal; the enormous
rake-offs were only the icing on the cake.

Following his tenure as U.S. permanent representative to the
UN in 1975, Daniel Patrick Moynihan described in humorous
terms what he called the "squalid circus" at Turtle Bay, location of
the UN's headquarters in New York:

Envision the British Home Office of 1900 enlarged five
hundredfold, teeming with the incompetent appointees
of decadent peers and corrupt borough councilors, infil-
trated and near to immobilized by agents of the Black
Hand, Sinn Fein, and Rosicrucians. . . . That approxi-
mates the United Nations Secretariat three quarters of a
century later.[108]

Alas, thirty years later, the picture is not much prettier.

In defense of the UN's record, Deputy Secretary General Shashi
Tharoor argues that "the UN's record of successes and failures is no
worse than that of most representative national institutions." And
he offers a litany of accomplishments:

The UN has brought humanitarian relief and helped people rebuild their countries from the ruins of war. It has challenged poverty, fought apartheid, protected the rights of children, promoted decolonization and democracy, and placed environmental and gender issues at the top of the world's agenda.[109]

But this list rings somewhat hollow. "Challeng[ing] poverty" is not the same as alleviating it. Nor is protecting "the rights of children" tantamount to protecting children. All the "fighting," "promoting," and "agenda-setting" amounts to little more than talk. In practice, the UN brings to whatever it undertakes a kind of bureaucratic inertia that would shame most democratic governments.

Propagating amoeba-like, the organization has created within itself more than one hundred separate entities. Their functioning was described by Rosemary Righter of the *Times* of London:

> The global organizations have accumulated a reputation for unreadable reports and working documents, for make-work programs and a scattershot approach to problems that deprives their work of impact, for consuming vast quantities of governments' time in the elaboration of declarations of blinding banality, for "strategies" that discredit the meaning of the word, and for duplicative effort beyond comprehension or control . . . Hundreds of senior UN officials do nothing except attend coordination meetings and "observe" the meetings of the councils and general conferences of other agencies.[110]

This bureaucratic inertia was recognized in the recommendations of the secretary general's High-Level Panel on Threats, Challenges, and Change, which called for "a one-time review and replacement of personnel including through early retirement, to ensure that the Secretariat is staffed with the right people." This was necessary in order to enable the secretary general "to do his job properly."[111]

Part of the problem, however, may be the secretary general himself. In the 1990s, Kofi Annan headed the UN office of peace-keeping during its operations in Bosnia, Somalia, and Rwanda, whose tragic outcomes I have described. The *New Yorker's* Philip Gourevitch observed sardonically, "These operations would meet with catastrophe on Annan's watch, at the end of which he was elevated to Secretary-General."[112]

What is to explain this outcome? The simple answer is that secretaries general are chosen by politics, not for merit. Perhaps ironically in light of the clashes between Washington and Turtle Bay that have unfolded since, it was the United States that promoted Annan's candidacy in 1996 because it was eager to block another term for Boutros-Ghali, who was seen as both a poor leader and hostile to the United States. Annan may or may not have been Washington's ideal candidate, but he was a plausible alternative.

And if the politics of the UN system sometimes lead to the promotion of the undeserving, they can also lead to penalties for diligence. In the 1980s, Theo Van Boven, the director of the Commission on Human Rights, ignored the advice of Secretary General Perez de Cuellar and criticized by name governments that were guilty of egregious human rights violations. Apparently for this indiscretion, Perez de Cuellar refused to renew his appointment.

The sexual and financial scandals that dog the UN are themselves only a kind of metaphor for a larger corruption of political principle that makes a mockery of the lofty sentiments of the charter. When Rwandan Hutus launched into wholesale slaughter of their Tutsi countrymen in 1994, Michael Barnett, a political scientist from the University of Wisconsin, found himself seconded to the U.S. mission to the UN, where he was assigned to work on African affairs. In a small but eye-opening book, he recorded his shock at what he saw around him. "UN staff," he writes, ". . . acted in ways that suggest that they believed the organization's interests (and perhaps their own careers) would be better served by remaining distant." The organization was "so consumed by fears of its own mortality that it had little evident compassion for those on the ground."[113]

Human Rights

Nowhere is the UN's broken moral compass more vividly on display than in the UN Commission on Human Rights. Year after year, many of the governments on the short list cited annually by Freedom House as the "worst of the worst" human rights violators (those receiving the poorest possible freedom score of 7 or 6.5 on its scale of 1 to 7) secure seats on the commission. In 2002 half the members of this rogues' gallery made it on; in 2003, a majority—five out of nine—did so. Its chairmanship has, at various times, been held by the likes of Poland and Bulgaria when they were under Soviet-imposed Communist rule, Libya, the Ukrainian Soviet Socialist Republic, the Byelorussian Soviet Socialist Republic, Afghanistan, and Uganda, as well as a variety of lesser autocracies.

At each annual sitting of the commission numerous resolutions are adopted, usually about ninety, asserting in careful detail all manner of human rights. These are both traditional and novel, and pertain to a nearly limitless range of demographic and sociological groups, from migrants, missing persons, juvenile offenders, conscientious objectors, and people with HIV/AIDS to more familiar victims, such as indigenous peoples and the "African diaspora." They include an exhaustive litany spelled out long ago in the UN's Universal Declaration of Human Rights and its twin covenants, on civil and political rights and on economic, social, and cultural rights. In addition, bows are paid to the "rights" to peace, development, and debt relief, along with such obscurities as the right "to establish cultural industries that [are] viable and competitive at national and international levels";[114] the right to "sound management of unwanted stocks of hazardous wastes";[115] and more or less any other right that anyone present at one of the sessions can dream up.

There is no cost to adding another resolution—and no practical effect from having done so. When the time comes to examine specific cases, rarely is a word of criticism aimed at the most brutal tyrannies, no matter how flagrantly they may traduce the most elementary of rights. This impunity applies evenhandedly to regimes of the left and the right, so long as they are influential. For instance, although each year the commission endorses virtually without dissent as full a panoply of resolutions on women's rights as any Western feminist might desire, it never breathes a word of criticism of, say, Saudi Arabia, where, among myriad other disabilities, women are not allowed to drive automobiles or travel without the express authorization of their husbands or fathers or brothers or adult sons or some responsible member of the superior sex. Also escaping censure is China, whose Communist government has murdered millions of its own citizens in such escapades as the "Cultural Revolution." Every year but one that America has tried to put China's record on the agenda for discussion, it has been voted down. The one year China was discussed, no motion of censure came near to passage.

In 2004, the American delegation made a concerted effort to secure a resolution criticizing the government of Sudan for the mass killings, rapes, and deportations underway in the Darfur region that have been labeled "genocide" by the House of Representatives and the president of the United States, among others. The U.S. strategy was to back a resolution tabled by the European Union, but then the EU, eager to avoid controversy, negotiated a watered-down text with the African Group (that is, the caucus of African members), which was acting reflexively, as usual, to shield one of its own from criticism. This text did not even authorize a "special rapporteur" to examine the conditions in Darfur, a usual method by which the commission exerts its moral authority, such as it is. Human rights groups have criticized the UN Security Council for failing to mobilize a military force to rescue the people of Darfur; everyone is ready for someone else to do the job. But in the Commission on Human Rights, it was not possible to summon even unambiguous words on behalf of the victims.

While the world's worst offenders ordinarily get away without mention, each year perhaps a dozen less-powerful states that are unprotected within their own regions do come in for criticism, invariably in a single resolution, usually mild in tone. In recent years, Afghanistan, Burma, Burundi, Cambodia, Congo, Cuba, Equatorial Guinea, Haiti, Iran, Iraq, Rwanda, Somalia, Sudan, Uganda, Western Sahara, and Yugoslavia have undergone this experience. One country, however, comes in for special treatment. Each year anywhere from five to eight separate resolutions are adopted castigating Israel—for its actions in Gaza and the West Bank; and in Jerusalem; and in Lebanon; and in the Golan; and in Israel proper.

Unlike any of the others, the blizzard of resolutions against Israel is couched in harsh language. So far do these denunciations go that each year of the last several, the commission has "affirmed the legitimate right of the Palestinian people to resist the Israeli occupation." To dispel any doubt about the import of the term "resist," the resolutions invoke the authority of General Assembly Resolution 37/43 of December 3, 1982, which proclaims "the legitimacy of the struggle of peoples against foreign occupation by all available means, including armed struggle."[116] As everyone understood then and now, the last six words mean terrorism. And by such means, says the resolution, "the Palestinian people is fulfilling . . . one of the goals and purposes of the United Nations."[117]

UN publications on human rights blithely boast that "over the years the secretariat has fine-tuned its management of this vital issue,"[118] yet the High-Level Panel acknowledged that the Commission on Human Rights had been "undermined by eroding credibility and professionalism,"[119] and Kofi Annan said that this had become so bad that it "casts a shadow on the reputation of the United Nations system as a whole."[120] The panel recommended making the commission a committee of the whole, in effect submerging it into the General Assembly.

But the UN's problems with the issue of human rights are not limited to the activities of the commission. In 2001, an official preparatory meeting hosted by Iran for a UN human rights conference openly barred Jewish, Bahai, and Kurdish nongovernmental organizations (NGOs).[121] Such blatant racial and religious discrimination is all too common in the world, but only in the UN is it perpetrated in the name of human rights.

Some Nations Are Less Equal than Others

The disreputable record of the Commission on Human Rights regarding Israel is only the tip of the iceberg. In a thousand ways the UN acts as a kind of permanent pogrom against the Jewish state to which, ironically, the UN itself gave birth. Alone among UN member-states, Israel was excluded from membership in any regional caucus. In 2000, the United States fought to secure a partial and attenuated membership for it in the caucus called WEOG, the Western Europe and Others Group. The membership was temporary, and it applied only to those UN bodies that are headquartered in New York, not the numerous UN agencies based in Geneva and other locales, meaning, for one thing, that Israel continued to be excluded from ever sitting on the Commission on Human Rights. And even with regard to the New York structures, the bargain excluded the right to run for the Security Council until the year 2006.

There are, moreover, no fewer than three special bodies of the UN, funded to the tune of 5 million dollars a year,[122] devoted exclusively to propagation of Palestinian grievances—meaning the denunciation of Israel. They are the Special Committee to Investigate Israeli Practices Affecting the Human Rights of the Palestinian People and Other Arabs of the Occupied Territories, the Committee on the Exercise of the Inalienable Rights of the Palestinian People, and the Division on Palestinian Rights. There is not a single equivalent body for any other suffering nationality.

The largest fiscal allocation goes to the Division of Palestinian Rights, the essence of whose largely "educational" work is to call into question Israel's right to exist. The cornerstone of its approach is presented in a book-length study it published in 1990 entitled *The Origins and Evolution of the Palestine Problem 1917–1988*. Therein it is explained that "the Balfour Declaration . . . can be considered the root of the problem of Palestine."[123] That declaration laid down the principle of the establishment of a homeland for the Jews in Palestine, and it was incorporated into the mandate over that territory given to the United Kingdom under the League of Nations.

Readers of this particular UN study, however, are led to see that the mandate itself was in all likelihood illegal:

> It is clear that by failing to consult the Palestinian peo-
> ple in the decision on the future of their country, the
> victorious Powers ignored not only the principle of self-
> determination that they themselves had endorsed, but
> also the provisions of Article 22 of the League's Covenant.
> . . . Several authorities of international law . . . have ques-
> tioned the validity of the Mandate.[124]

The study goes on to quote at length from one such skeptic, Professor Henry Cattan. It does not present any view to the contrary—that is, in defense of the legitimacy of the mandate. And it rather slyly passes Cattan off as simply an authority on international law, without mentioning that he is a lifelong Palestinian activist who was a member of the Arab Higher Committee during World War II.[125]

Glossing over the decision of the Arab states to thwart the birth of a Jewish state by means of military invasion upon the expiration of the mandate, the UN study discusses the 1948 war under the heading "Zionist Policies of Territorial Expansion." It explains that "this territorial expansion by the use of force resulted in a large-scale exodus of refugees from the areas of hostilities," as if it were the Jews who initiated the violence.[126] Subsequent history is treated in a similar highly tendentious manner. In short, the Division of Palestinian Rights serves to put the UN's imprimatur on an extremely one-sided account of the conflict. Since the 1993 Oslo Accords, the division proclaims itself in support of the peace process, but it is hard to see how any peace could be reached on the premise that one side consists only of aggrieved victims and the other of cunning despoilers.

Palestinian grievances are not only championed by the UN; they are even cultivated by it. Everywhere else in the world, the UN attempts to succor those in flight from violence and persecution through the High Commissioner for Refugees. But for Palestinians there exists a special UN agency, the UN Relief and Works Agency for Palestine Refugees (UNRWA). Anywhere else in the world, the UN counts as refugees individuals who themselves fled from conflict; but for the Palestinians, the children and grandchildren and all "descendants," as UNRWA puts it, of those who fled are also somehow considered "refugees." While the High Commissioner for Refugees employs a staff of five thousand for a target population of refugees, asylum-seekers, and "others of concern" that it estimates to number 17 million, UNRWA employs twenty-five thousand for a target population that it counts as "above four million."

UNRWA says that the overwhelming majority of its employees are Palestinians, and it turns out that some of them are also members of terrorist groups. Some have used their positions to facilitate acts of terror, such as Nahed Rashid Ahmed Attalah, who admitted in court to using his UN car and travel permit to transport arms, explosives, and terrorists.[127] When, in a 2004 interview on Canadian television, UNRWA's commissioner general Peter Hansen was asked about this, he replied: "I am sure there are Hamas members on the UNRWA payroll, and I don't see that as a crime."[128]

The most important difference between the High Commissioner for Refugees and UNRWA is that the goal of the former is to aid refugees in finding safe places to settle and build normal lives, while the role of the latter is just the opposite. It is to maximize the number of refugees and to maintain their status so that they can be the cutting edge of the struggle against Israel. The editor of the Palestinian newspaper *Al-Fajr* explained the underlying political, rather than humanitarian, mission: "As long as UNRWA exists, it is a sign that the UN supports the Palestinian people. . . . The camps, the schools, the clinics are a symbol. UNRWA's work will be over when the Palestinian state is created, and not before."[129]

In 2001 the UN's special conference against racism in Durban turned into a hate-fest against Israel and Jews so raw that Secretary of State Colin Powell felt compelled to withdraw the U.S. delegation. The official resolutions contained one-sided attacks on Israel. Aside from the imbalance, the issue itself was germane only by a stretch. By the same stretch, many other conflicts around the world might have been apropos (Russian–Chechen, Armenian–Azerbaijani, Turkish–Kurd, and Hutu–Tutsi, among others), but none was mentioned. When a resolution deploring prejudice was adopted, the delegates turned down a proposal to include anti-Semitism among the forms of prejudice mentioned.

But the bigotry displayed in the official session was surpassed by that displayed at the officially recognized NGO forum that proceeded in parallel. As Congressman Tom Lantos, one of the U.S. delegates, described it,

> Each day, [Palestinian and Islamist] groups organized anti-Israeli and anti-Semitic rallies around the meetings, attracting thousands. One flyer which was widely distributed showed a photograph of Hitler and the question "What if I had won?" The answer: "There would be NO Israel." At a press conference held by Jewish NGOs to discuss their concerns with the direction the conference was taking, an accredited NGO, the Arab Lawyers Union, distributed a booklet filled with anti-Semitic caricatures frighteningly like those seen in the Nazi hate literature printed in the 1930s.[130]

While the UN has had a hard time seeing anything damnable in anti-Semitism, it has had no such difficulty in spying the evil in Zionism. In 1975, the General Assembly adopted a resolution condemning Zionism as a form of racism.[131] Moynihan lamented the American delegation's failure "to understand the willingness of the Arabs simply to buy themselves a majority."[132] Perhaps it was not the Arabs' willingness to buy that deserved most comment, but the other members' willingness to be bought. After the disappearance of the Soviet bloc, which had supported this odious resolution, the United States succeeded in winning its repeal in 1991, but the underlying animus of the General Assembly toward Israel, whether heartfelt or bought and paid for, continued. The same year that it repealed "Zionism as Racism," the assembly passed no fewer than thirty-four resolutions denouncing Israel, as if the world had few other problems and none of equal weight or urgency. Each year, indeed, an amazing disproportion of the resolutions voted on in the General Assembly are devoted to this subject, often as many as 20 percent. (This proportion excludes the large number of anodyne consensus resolutions on which no vote is taken.)

The mechanism that the United States launched in 1950 with its *Uniting for Peace* resolution has led to special "emergency" sessions being called ten times. Of these, six have been aimed against Israel, and even this statistic—six out of ten—understates the case. The seventh session, devoted to "Palestine," convened not once, but six different times between July 1980 and September 1982, and the tenth session, devoted to "Occupied East Jerusalem and the rest of the Occupied Palestinian Territory," has met ten times since it was first convened in 1997 and may be reconvened *ad infinitum.*

The Arabs have unique leverage with which they can make the UN say whatever they want (except in the Security Council, where the U.S. veto has prevented that). The 22-nation Arab League constitutes a decisive bloc within the 56-nation Organization of the Islamic Conference, which is decisive in turn in the 115-nation Non-Aligned Movement (NAM), which constitutes nearly two-thirds of the UN and is the organization's dominant bloc. This makes it easy for the Arabs to vent their anger in the most extreme terms and have it validated by the UN—which they do repeatedly.

The temptation to exercise this power may be irresistible, but it is a form of self-indulgence that is as damaging to themselves as it is to Israel. If there is ever to be an end to the long, brutal conflict between Israelis and Arabs, it will require a measure of empathy on both sides. Each will have to recognize the sufferings of the other and accommodate the needs that grow from them. The UN's one-sidedness makes it harder to reach the compromises that would free both sides from their mutual death grip. Thus does the UN serve as an obstacle to peace in the Middle East.

Moreover, the endless campaign against Israel in the UN has made it impossible to gather a world consensus against terrorism. Indeed, as Israel's former ambassador to the UN, Dore Gold, has demonstrated in *Tower of Babble: How the United Nations Has Created*

Global Chaos, the UN itself acted as a kind of hothouse in which the current plague of international terrorism was cultivated. Beginning in the 1970s, when the terror epidemic took root, the General Assembly went out of its way to affirm that groups fighting for their "right to self-determination and independence" had a legitimate right to use "all the necessary means at their disposal."[133] In 1974, more than a dozen years before he had even nominally renounced terrorism, Yasir Arafat appeared before the General Assembly. Five times during his speech he boasted of the Palestinians' "armed struggle," meaning attacks on Israeli civilians, and to dramatize the point he displayed a holster on his belt as he stood on the UN podium. Yet far from being chastised for the terrorism that was his stock in trade, he received a hero's welcome.

Eventually, however, as terrorism around the globe increased, so did pressure for the UN to respond to it. Thus, in 1997, a UN committee was tasked with drafting a "comprehensive convention on international terrorism." It has been stalled since day one on the issue of "defining" terrorism. But what is the mystery? At bottom everyone understands what terrorism is: the deliberate targeting of civilians. The Islamic Conference, however, has insisted that terrorism must be defined not by the nature of the act but by its purpose. In this view, any act committed in the cause of "national liberation," no matter how bestial, nor how random or defenseless the victims, cannot be considered terrorism. This boils down to saying that terrorism on behalf of bad causes is bad, but terrorism on behalf of good causes is good. Obviously, anyone who takes such a position is not against terrorism at all—only against bad causes.

In the wake of the 9/11 attacks on America, Kofi Annan attempted to break the impasse. He threw his weight behind a new UN convention condemning terrorism, but it was blocked by the Islamic Conference, which insisted "that anti-Israeli militants be exempted from the pact's provisions."[134] In 2004, after Chechen separatists seized a school in Beslan and massacred hundreds of children, Russia introduced a resolution condemning "terrorism" at the Security Council, which passed unanimously. But spokesmen for the Islamic members of the council made clear that in their interpretation it did not apply to Palestinians or other "freedom-fighters," since by definition nothing they do could constitute "terrorism." As Pakistan's representative put it, "We ought not, in our desire to confront terrorism, erode the principle of the legitimacy of national resistance that we have upheld for 50 years." And he said he was "happy" with the resolution: "It doesn't open any new doors."[135]

Also in 2004, the High-Level Panel on Threats, Challenges, and Change attempted to break the impasse on terrorism. After bowing to the terrorists' rationalizations by serving up a doleful litany of "root causes" of terrorism, including "foreign occupation,"[136] it nonetheless proposed a clear definition of terrorism, to wit:

> any action . . . that is intended to cause death or serious bodily harm to civilians or non-combatants, when the purpose of such an act, by its nature or context, is to intimidate a population, or to compel a Government or an international organization to do or to abstain from doing any act.[137]

In his March 2005 report, Secretary General Annan strongly endorsed this language, challenging the familiar rationalizations for terrorism with a frankness unusual in the UN:

> It is time to set aside debates on so-called "State terrorism." The use of force by States is already thoroughly regulated under international law. And the right to resist occupation . . . cannot include the right to deliberately kill or maim civilians. I believe this proposal has clear moral force, and I strongly urge world leaders to unite behind it and to conclude a comprehensive convention on terrorism.[138]

If such a convention is agreed to, it would mark an important about-face for the UN on the subject of terrorism.

Combating Poverty

The failures to uphold peace and security and the moral inversion represented by the UN's history on issues of human rights, terrorism, and Israel do not, alas, exhaust the list of areas in which the UN has failed or been downright harmful. It has also helped to perpetuate global poverty. This, of course, was the very opposite of its intention. As third-world nations came to make up a majority of the UN's membership, they naturally drove the body to focus on their own problems. Thus, UN forums became a major arena of agitation for the liquidation of the last vestiges of Western colonialism. It is possible that this process would have been rougher and bloodier had the UN not provided this framework.

But the politics of anti-Western resentment that gained such momentum within the UN proved self-defeating. In 1961 the General Assembly declared the "United Nations Development Decade." This was followed three years later by the United Nations Conference on Trade and Development. Initially a conference, later in 1964 UNCTAD was made a permanent organ of the General Assembly. Secretary General U Thant appointed Raul Prebisch as secretary general of UNCTAD.

Prebisch, an Argentine economist, was a pioneer in development economics. As head of the UN's Economic Commission for Latin America, he had formulated what came to be called "dependency theory." The essence of this theory was that what held poor countries back was their intercourse with rich countries, which would inevitably be an "unequal exchange" because the rich held all the advantages. He recommended that poor countries erect trade barriers and practice "import-substitution." He explained his philosophy: "If I was to single out one thing which slowed down the pace of progress in my time . . . it would be this conviction about . . . the sanctity of market forces."[139] The better alternative, he said, was "collective rationality," another term for economic planning.

The first UNCTAD conference also gave birth to the so-called Group of Seventy-Seven (G-77), a bloc of developing states within the UN (originally 77 in number, but 132 as of 2004) with the declared purpose of enabling "the developing world to articulate and promote its collective economic interests and enhance its joint negotiating capacity on all major international economic issues in the United Nations system."[140] The Group of Seventy-Seven advanced a program demanding a New International Economic Order (NIEO), and in the early 1970s it succeeded in winning the endorsement of this concept by UNESCO (United Nations Educational, Cultural and Scientific Organization).

The main ideas of the NIEO were sketched in the Charter of Economic Rights and Duties of States adopted by the General Assembly in 1974.[141] It called for "more rational and equitable international economic relations" and "structural changes in the world economy." These would include "increas[ing] net flows of real resources to the developing countries from all sources," and on "better terms and conditions" than in the past. It also demanded an enlarged system of "generalized non-reciprocal . . . tariff preferences to the developing countries"; mechanisms to ensure "stable, equitable and remunerative prices for primary goods"; and recognition of the right of primary product producers to form cartels, free from any "economic or political measures that would limit" them.[142]

The charter stressed that "every state has and shall freely exercise full permanent sovereignty, including possession, use and disposal, over all its wealth, natural resources and economic activities." In particular, it proclaimed the right of states

> to nationalize, expropriate or transfer ownership of foreign property, in which case appropriate compensation should be paid . . . taking into account . . . relevant laws and regulations and all circumstances that the State considers pertinent. In any case where the question of compensation gives rise to a controversy, it shall be settled under the domestic law of the nationalizing state.[143]

While asserting so forcefully the rights of states, the charter contained not a word about rights of human individuals.

Just as individual states had a right of expropriation, so the community of states was given the right to appropriate to itself the ocean floor and subsoil, to ensure that "the benefits derived therefrom are shared equitably by all States, taking into account the particular interests and needs of developing countries." In sum, the entire charter was a formula for state domination of national economies and international economics.[144]

Both from UNCTAD and the NIEO, the guidance that the UN gave to developing countries pointed toward a socialist or statist path to development. It encouraged the belief that poor countries were poor because rich countries were rich, and much the same for the differences among people. The prescriptions this led to were to reduce economic relations with the developed countries, demand more donations from them, and maximize government's role in their own economies. It is hard to think of more destructive advice. Yet the newly independent nations had few qualified experts or experienced leaders of their own. The advice of UNCTAD and the NIEO came to them as the voice of authority. Nay, better, it was the voice of their tribune. The G-77 was like their labor union, and Prebisch their hero. As Richard Gardner, one of the American representatives to UNCTAD, put it, "The poor countries were looking for a dynamic exponent of their interests—and they found one in the charismatic figure of Dr. Raul Prebisch . . . whose theoretical formulations and policy prescriptions fit perfectly their economic and political interests."[145]

Urged on by the UN, the majority of developing countries adopted socialist strategies. The massive additional transfers of wealth from the developed world never arrived, which ought not to have been a surprise. But even if they had, it would have made little difference. Bitter experience teaches that outside donations to fettered economies disappear with hardly a trace. No developing country received more foreign aid per capita than Tanzania during the decades of rule by socialist Julius Nyerere, and the net result was sheer stagnation.[146] So, too, with most of the nearly sixty other developing countries that embraced such policies.[147] They lost many years before the successful examples of the "little tigers" of

East Asia demonstrated that the best route for poor countries ran in the opposite direction from the one the UN had told them to take—namely, to maximize intercourse with rich countries.

3

Some Areas of Success

Peacekeeping

While the UN's failures are more numerous and easier to enumerate, the organization has some successes to its credit. As against the body's failures in various conflict situations, its peacekeeping efforts in Namibia, Cambodia, El Salvador, Mozambique, Eastern Slavonia, and East Timor are generally regarded as having achieved their missions. These were cases of agreed transfers of authority, or where previously warring parties had reached a settlement but still felt distrust of one another. UN peacekeepers were not there to enforce agreements but to provide good offices trusted by all sides, verifying to each that the other was keeping its side of the bargain, or to maintain order and safety during a transition. In addition, the UN generally played a short-term administrative role that included, as a RAND study summarized it, "disarmament, demobilization, and reintegration; encouraging political reconciliation; holding democratic elections; and overseeing the inauguration of a new national government."[1]

An important exception to the generalization that these peacekeeping operations proceeded in environments that were already peaceful was Cambodia, where the peacekeepers found they had a tougher assignment. Although the four main parties to the conflict reached agreement to hold elections, the most murderous, the Khmer Rouge, soon reversed itself. It announced its refusal to participate and attempted to disrupt the voting through violence and

73

threats. Thus, the peacekeepers had to guard the balloting by force as best they could, and on the whole they succeeded admirably, aided by the surprising determination of the Cambodian populace not to be intimidated from voting. Another exception was East Timor, where UN forces came ashore in the wake of serious mayhem that had claimed a thousand lives. But the murderous militias and Indonesian military forces responsible for the killing apparently received orders to back down in the face of the formidable Australian-led international force, and it was able to occupy the territory without taking any casualties.[2]

In assessing these missions, the RAND study argues that the UN has a "better . . . success rate" at "nation-building" than the United States, a conclusion that is sure to be widely repeated.[3] But the cases compared are dissimilar, and many are ongoing. For instance, RAND counts Afghanistan and Iraq as U.S. failures because they have not yet reached their goals.

It is also hard to understand how RAND categorizes cases, since the United States and the UN both were present in many of these situations. In one case, RAND places El Salvador in the UN column and rates it a success. But the UN was active in El Salvador only during the relatively easy endgame, after the guerrillas had agreed to lay down arms, whereas the United States spent years nurturing a "third force" in that country between the military and the guerrillas, which was the key to the success of nation-building.

On the other hand, RAND counts Somalia as a nation-building failure, as it surely was, and places it in the U.S. column. It is true that the military operation that ended in debacle for U.S. forces in Mogadishu was planned and commanded by Americans. But the idea of going beyond famine relief to nation-building in Somalia belonged to the UN, not the United States, although the United States went along. Thus, the strained comparison that RAND goes out of its way to make seems intended for polemical purposes.

UN peacekeepers have also been deployed in countries in turmoil, mostly in Africa—notably Sierra Leone, Liberia, and Congo—where they have had, at best, modest accomplishments. Although the UN forces have not been strong enough to impose peace in any of these places, their presence in at least some has ameliorated problems. (In Sierra Leone, the UN intervention was initially a fruitless humiliation in which, as in Bosnia, the peacekeepers themselves were taken hostage; but a more robust British-led force operating at first outside of UN command had a better result.)

Unarmed or lightly armed UN forces have also been deployed along troubled borders, such as between Ethiopia and Eritrea, Israel and Lebanon, Israel and Syria, and Greek and Turkish Cyprus, where their presence has helped dampen violence.

The deficiencies of UN peacekeeping efforts must be judged in light of the rapid proliferation of such missions with the end of the Cold War. In the era from 1948 to 1988, there was a total of fifteen UN peacekeeping missions. In the next fifteen years there were another forty-four. Without superpower rivalry, it became much more feasible politically to introduce UN forces. This rapid upsurge in demand, however, outstripped the institution's capacities and the numbers of properly prepared troops. Hence, UN missions were typically undermanned and underequipped due to the reluctance of the advanced countries to supply soldiers for such operations. According to the UN Department of Peacekeeping Operations, the total number of Americans serving UN peacekeeping missions on May 31, 2005 was ten (as well as 19 military observers and upwards of 300 civilian police).[4] All too often, the countries that do contribute troops bring to the table much less in the way of military capability. This is the key factor that has prevented an effective response to, for example, the humanitarian catastrophe in Darfur in recent times.

Notwithstanding the severe limitations, the UN does provide a useful framework for legitimizing peacekeeping missions, usually in situations in which no major power has a vested interest, and the stakes in human life are large.

Regulatory Agencies

Any enumeration of the UN's essential functions must begin with its regulatory agencies. The International Telecommunications Union provides the protocols that make it easy to call or send e-mail any place in the world. It also helps to manage the radio-frequency spectrum essential to the smooth functioning not only of radio and television broadcasting, but also cell phones and pagers, aircraft and maritime navigation systems, communications satellites, and more. The ITU, originally called the International Telegraph Union, was founded eighty years before the UN, in 1865. The International Civil Aviation Organization, founded in 1944, establishes procedures for international air travel and sets safety standards for various aspects of aviation, including training, operations, and maintenance. The Universal Postal Union, dating from 1874, provides a system of mutual compensation that makes it possible to drop a letter in a box in one country and have it delivered in another. Over the first several years of the UN's existence, these once-autonomous agencies affiliated with the UN.

In addition, the humanitarian work of the UN's various specialized agencies such as WHO, The United Nations Children's Fund (UNICEF), the World Food Program, and the High Commissioner for Refugees is widely acknowledged to have provided lifesaving assistance to people in need. WHO's timely intervention helped to stem the spread of Sudden Acute Respiratory Syndrome (SARS) in 2002–03. SARS might have burgeoned into an epidemic causing untold fatalities, fanned by the irresponsible reaction of Communist Chinese authorities more interested in saving face than saving lives. Instead, the outbreak was contained, and its death toll numbered "only" in the hundreds. WHO has also played an important role in eradicating smallpox and in virtually eliminating polio (although the latter disease has made a tragic return in Muslim countries, due to propagation of the rumor that polio vaccine was part of a Western conspiracy to make Muslims infertile[5]). It can claim credit for important advances against tuberculosis and other diseases.

UNICEF has brought health services to countless children. It claims it provides vaccines to forty percent of the world's children, and has thrown its weight behind equalization of educational opportunities for girls in countries where this is far from the norm. In scores of poor countries, especially those in turmoil such as

Sudan in recent times, the World Food Program provides rations for schoolchildren and others living with hunger.

The High Commissioner succored refugees from the calamitous violence in northern Iraq, Sudan, Congo, Rwanda, and the former Yugoslavia. It functioned best in the 1990s, when the post was filled by Sadako Ogata. She replaced Jean-Pierre Hocké, who was forced to leave office after revelations that he had diverted funds from an account for refugee education to pay for first-class travel and entertainment.[6] Ogata instead set a tone of dedication and seriousness; on some occasions during her tenure, when governments and the UN's own political arms were downplaying disasters so as not to be embarrassed in their inertia, reporters relied on the HCR for unvarnished accounts of the direness of these situations. Alas, she was succeeded by Ruud Lubbers, under whom clouds of scandal again surrounded the agency.

The UN's premier advocate in America, Timothy Wirth, head of the UN Foundation, likes to say that he is not concerned with the activities of the Security Council or General Assembly and other political bodies, whose work is hard to defend, but with the humanitarian agencies that "account for 80 percent of the UN's budget." Much of their work is noble, but it also has been marred by the UN's characteristic bureaucratism and political correctness.

For example, although UN officials gave the organization much credit for its response to the Indian Ocean catastrophe of 2004 ("The tsunami showed that only the UN has the universal legitimacy, capacity and credibility to lead in a truly global humanitarian emergency," wrote UN Undersecretary General Jan Egeland[7]), Australia's foreign minister, Alexander Downer, assessed the organization's performance more critically:

> The UN could not come and provide the immediate overnight assistance which was needed by people as a result of the tsunami. When it came to the tsunami, people were devastated and they couldn't wait a week or a month for assistance. They needed assistance immediately. The UN can't send planes to Sumatra, it

can't send ships to Sumatra, it doesn't have ships, and
so we and the Americans did it.[8]

Public health expert Roger Bate faults the WHO for not using
the insecticide DDT in combating malaria, settling for less effective
measures out of fear of DDT's ecological impact. Weakening anti-
malaria efforts for this reason is a faulty tradeoff, he argues, because
"it was the massive use of DDT in farming, not the small amounts
used in public-health, that caused the environmental problems."[9]

And many or most UN agencies have been tainted by the obses-
sive anti-Israelism that the Arab representatives inject into everything. Thus, in addition to its good work, the WHO makes the comic
declaration that "the Israeli occupation is a serious health problem."
Similarly obsessed, though not an Arab, is the leftist Swiss Jean
Ziegler, cofounder of an anti-American magazine, L'Empire (The
Empire), and also one of a group of self-described "intellectuals and
progressive militants" who gathered in Tripoli in 1989 to launch the
"Muammar Qaddafi Human Rights Prize," funded by the Libyan
government. Ziegler explained that the Qaddafi Prize was a riposte
to the Nobel Prize, which Ziegler denounced as a "perpetual humiliation to the Third World."[10] In 2002, the prize was awarded to
Roger Garaudy, who had previously been fined by a French court for
denying the Holocaust.

Ziegler himself was nominated to share the award with Garaudy
but turned down the honor on the grounds that "I could not accept
an award or distinction from any country because of my responsibilities at the United Nations."[11] Those responsibilities stem from
Ziegler's position as the UN's special rapporteur on the right to food.
Ziegler has used his office to polemicize against U.S. policies in
Afghanistan and Iraq and toward Cuba on the grounds that they
have been harmful to food consumption. Of all the countries in the
world, his office has focused its greatest attention by far on Israel,
for allegedly creating hunger among the Palestinians. He has gone
so far as to campaign for suspension of the EU's trade agreement
with Israel and for a boycott of the Caterpillar Company because it
sells bulldozers to Israel.

Despite the UN's disgraceful record on human rights, it has one fine recent accomplishment to its credit, namely the 2002 Arab Human Development Report, issued by the UN Development Program. This extraordinary document, "written for Arabs by Arabs"—that is, by a team of a few dozen Arab intellectuals—lamented three deficiencies in Arab life: lack of freedom, knowledge, and women's equality. It contributed significantly to the democratic ferment today shaking the Arab world, the one region that had remained untouched by the tide of democratization that had swept over the world from 1974 to 2004.

Although published in mid-2002, the Arab Human Development Report had been in the works since well before the infamous events of September 11, 2001, showing that democratic ideas had been crystallizing among an important group of Arab intellectuals before the United States embraced the strategy of promoting democracy in the Middle East. A second report, focusing on the knowledge deficit, followed in 2003 and a third, on the freedom deficit, in 2005. A fourth, on the deficit in women's participation, is scheduled for 2006. Although the second and third reports were larded over with ever larger doses of anti-American and anti-Israel rhetoric, still the gravamen of the reports is an urgency for the transformation of the Arab countries into free societies. That this message comes from Arabs and from the UN shows that it is not only Washington that is clamoring for democratization.

Finally, apart from any balancing scale of the UN's successes and failures, there is its intrinsic value. Tharoor puts it, "Multilateralism, of course, is not only a means but an end."[12] Philosophers and visionaries like Rousseau, Kant, and Thomas Paine pictured a world knitted much more closely together. For many of those who value the organization most highly, its performance is not the issue. Rather, as they see it, the UN stands, whatever its failings, as the first hopeful step on the vital journey to true world community. Last year its Panel of Eminent Persons on United Nations–Civil Society Relations declared that "the United Nations should accept a more explicit role in strengthening global governance and tackling the democratic deficits it is prone to [so as to] reshape democracy to make it more relevant to today's global realities and needs."[13] And as the television sage Walter Cronkite put it, "If we are to avoid catastrophe, a system of world order—preferably a system of world government—is mandatory. The proud nations someday will . . . yield up their precious sovereignty."[14]

4

Sources of Failure

However much it may remain a repository of hopes for a future when all men will more nearly feel toward one another as brothers, the record of the UN over its first sixty years shows more failures than successes. What is the cause of this sorry performance? Because the Cold War was such an obvious source of paralysis during the organization's first forty-five years, analysts have rarely probed further. But the Cold War has been over since 1989, and the organization's functioning has improved little. It is clear that other causes must be found.

The Non-Aligned Movement

The Soviet bloc was America's chief adversary, but it was not America's only nemesis in the UN, nor the only obstacle to our goals there. An equally destructive force was the so-called Non-Aligned Movement (NAM). Although not as squarely opposed to American interests as the Soviet Union was, the NAM was at odds with the United States more often than not, and within the UN it wielded more influence. According to the statistics published annually by the State Department, during the latter 1990s the members of the NAM collectively voted on the same side as the United States only 36 percent of the time (not counting anodyne motions adopted by consensus). However, starting in 2001 after the onset of the Palestinian "*intifada*," the September 11 attacks on America, and the declaration of a "war against terrorism," the chasm widened dramatically. NAM members' votes corresponded with those of the United States only 22 percent of the time in 2001 and 2002 and only 17 percent of the time in 2003.

In the earliest years of the UN, the United States enjoyed the support of the majority of members on most political questions, but as decolonization brought scores of new states into membership, the nations of the Third World became a powerful, often a dominant, force within the UN. Though nominally neutral between the two power blocs, the animating spirit of NAM from its establishment in 1961 (it was foreshadowed at the 1955 Bandung conference of Asian and African leaders) was hostility toward the West, and especially the United States. Its founding fathers were presidents Sukarno of Indonesia, Gamal Abdel Nasser of Egypt, Josip Tito of Yugoslavia, and India's prime minister Jawaharlal Nehru. All were socialists of one kind or another, and all leaned to the Soviet side in the Cold War, except, ironically, Tito, the one out-and-out Communist among them. His 1948 falling-out with Stalin had led him headlong into the arms of the West as far as security was concerned, although not in other respects. This tilt reached its climax at the 1979 NAM conference in Havana, where Tito fought to prevent the body from formally aligning itself with the Soviet Union.

NAM's anti-Western stance arose principally from two roots. The first was resentment over the history of colonial subjugation. The United States had been more a liberator of colonies than a subjugator, but still, as the leader of the West, it was held guilty by proxy of imperial depredations. The second cause was jealousy of the wealth of the West and the vastly superior competence of Western states. The two grievances were knitted together and reinforced by Marxist theories that third-world thinkers soaked up in equal measure from Soviet propagandists and Western intellectuals.

These theories lent a patina of logic to blaming the United States for Western imperialism by making imperialism out to be the inevitable outgrowth of capitalism, of which the United States was the apotheosis. They also bestowed moral legitimacy on third-world envy by teaching that poor countries owed their poverty to the wealth of rich countries.

Perhaps the term "envy" puts too psychological a twist on it. The socialist ideas of the NAM leaders caused them to focus more on the distribution of wealth than its production, to see economics as a zero-sum game. The way to raise their countries out of poverty was to compel the countries that had the wealth to hand it over. And this meant above all the Western countries, either because they sensed that the Soviet bloc had less to give or because they knew that the West was a softer touch.

Because of their military weakness, the nonaligned countries cannot deserve much of the blame for the failure of the UN to keep the peace. But NAM contributed mightily to many of the organization's other derelictions. For example, the rank hypocrisy of the Commission on Human Rights is owing largely to the influence of NAM, whether exercised formally or informally. Usually, a majority of the commission's fifty-three members are also members of NAM. Most of the caucusing takes place in regional blocs, rather than as NAM, but the spirit of developing-world-versus-the-West propounded by NAM infuses the caucuses. Thus, for example, in 2004 the African bloc decided to oppose any significant criticism of ethnic cleansing in Darfur, Sudan, even though the perpetrators are Arab Africans while the victims are blacks with whom most African states might presumably feel more affinity. Once this decision was taken, the other developing countries fell in line with the Africans.

Similarly, the UN's grotesque scapegoating of Israel results from the solidarity that the Arab and Muslim states count on from the other NAM members. (In its first eighteen years of existence, NAM never criticized one of its own, but then in 1979, Egypt did the unforgivable. It made peace with Israel, and for this NAM broke precedent with a rousing condemnation of Egypt's perfidy. A motion of expulsion from NAM nearly passed, but instead Egypt was merely put on probation.) And, as I have already described, the UN's propagation of crippling statist economics in developing countries is also due largely to the influence of NAM.

European Anti-Americanism

Although NAM's overwhelming numbers give it an apparent lock on the UN, this might be counterbalanced by the political weight of the Western states if they acted in concert. But the European governments have no stomach for confrontation with the Third World. On the contrary, as Rosemary Righter describes it, rather than defend liberal principles the Western Europeans have responded to the third-world bloc by reminding themselves that "morality resides more in the acceptance of difference than in insistence on universal values" and "that the West's moral capital rests in part on its readiness to acknowledge its imperfections." As a result of this self-flagellation, she adds,

> There is a reluctance to admit that the erosion of the Charter's principles might weaken international cooperation. Insistence on defending "mere words" [as the United States has tried to do] appears to most European diplomats arrogant, and doomed to failure. This difference of perspective has been at times so marked as to give the impression that "European policy," insofar as there is such a thing, is largely about mitigating the excesses in UN forums of Europe's embarrassing friend, the United States.[1]

Thus does Europe collude in letting Khartoum off the hook on Darfur, exempting China from criticism in the Human Rights Commission, and passing euphemistic affirmations of the "right" of Palestinians to engage in suicide bombing.

One important exception to this pattern was the support several other Western governments gave the United States in its resistance to the New World Information and Communication Order first propounded by UNESCO and then endorsed by the General Assembly in 1985. The simple idea behind this "new order" was that governments should cooperate against unregulated news media or other means of communication. Dictatorial regimes were feeling frustrated by the fact that even though they could control their own national news organizations, they still found themselves subject to criticism or uncensored coverage by foreign or multinational news organizations. The "new order" was designed to suppress this practice by

subjecting all of the world's communications media to intergovern-
mental control. The salience of the issue of free speech and the sensitivity of news organizations to this issue (as well as the sensitivity of
Western governments to the feelings of news organizations) ensured
strong resistance to the idea. But still the West was not completely
united. French culture minister Jack Lang denounced the freedom of
U.S. information media to report on and in third-world countries as
"the freedom of the fox in the barnyard."[2]

Lang is a particularly extreme anti-American, but France has a
broad policy of counteracting American "hyperpuissance," which
leads it repeatedly to oppose U.S. positions both within and without the UN. At the outset of the crisis in Bosnia, France proposed
that it be handled by the Western European Union, a paper organization at best. The only conceivable reason for invoking it was to
have an alternative to NATO, so as to keep the United States
away. At every subsequent turn, France tilted toward the Serbs—
shielding them, for example, from the loss of Yugoslavia's UN
seat—and blocked efforts to relieve their Muslim victims. In Rwanda,
France armed and trained the Hutu military that participated in the
genocide of Tutsis, and there were accusations in the French press
that this aid continued even after the genocide had begun.[3]

Moreover, there is evidence that France coached Secretary General Boutros Boutros-Ghali to present misleadingly low-key accounts
of what was transpiring in Rwanda even while covering up reports
from the field that made clear that genocide was in progress.[4] Regarding Iraq, France worked assiduously in the Security Council to
weaken sanctions and to accommodate the Iraqi regime's demands
about the nature of arms inspections and the protocols under which
the oil-for-food program would be administered.

And, of course, in the final showdown between the United
States and Iraq, France persuaded the U.S. administration to work
through the Security Council to force Saddam Hussein to comply
with his obligations to furnish proof of having liquidated his mass-
destruction weapons programs. Then, when Saddam defied the
Security Council's demands, France took the lead in blocking a resolution authorizing military action.

France often uses the UN to try to cut the United States down to size, even where this means damaging goals or principles that France nominally shares with America. For example, in 2001, the European Union colluded with Cuba and China in the Economic and Social Council to ensure that the United States was defeated in its candidacy for a renewed seat on the Commission on Human Rights, even though the predictable result of this was that the world's dictators became safer from criticism by the commission than ever before. (The Western Europe and Others Group to which the United States belongs was entitled to three seats, which ordinarily would have gone to the United States plus two others. On this occasion, however, the EU nominated three candidates, making a total of four nominees for the three seats and thus forcing a vote by the full body, which the United States lost.) Most of the wheeling and dealing was secret, but there is little doubt that France was an instigator.

Lack of Accountability

Obviously, the United States is bound to be most sensitive to the abuse of the UN by states pursuing anti-American objectives, but there are other causes of the UN's poor record that are apparent without looking through the prism of American interests. The most profound is the organization's lack of accountability.

To begin with, many of the governments that constitute the UN are dictatorships. This includes one of the permanent members of the Security Council, China, while a second permanent member, Russia, is now more like a dictatorship than a democracy; in its May 2005 survey of freedom in the world, Freedom House downgraded Russia from the rank of "partly free" to "not free."[5] Dictators are not accountable to their own subjects for the generality of their actions, much less for their role in the UN.

The composition of the UN has been improved by the spread of democracy in recent decades. Most of its 191 member-states—some 118—had elected governments, according to the 2004 survey by

Freedom House. Of these, 88 were judged to be "free," meaning that they not only had elections but also a free press, independent courts, rule of law, and other aspects of a fully democratic system.[6]

The problems of UN accountability, however, are not limited to dictatorial governments. Even from the perspective of democracies, the UN is so distant that there is little connection between the international body and the citizens of the member-states. It was a premise of the American Constitution, which spawned the world's first modern democracy, that government should be kept close to the citizen. The Tenth Amendment reserved to the states and the people all powers that were not explicitly "delegated" to federal authority. Some decisions had to be made or functions performed at a more remote level, but these were to be assigned with care, for fear that the more distant the government, the less certain would be its responsiveness to the citizen.

This axiom applies all the more forcefully at the international level. How many citizens of democracies know how their "representatives" vote in the UN or what issues are before it? How many care? The answer is that the practical procedures by which even the citizens of democracies can express their wishes about what the UN ought to do are few and weak. And this is only the beginning of the problem.

The remoteness of the UN from the citizens of any country is compounded by its opacity. The secretariat's staff of eighteen thousand is like a government. It enjoys a kind of diplomatic status and extraterritoriality. UN employees are often exempt from taxes and entitled to legal immunity. The "government" they are part of, however, is not elected by any population or public constituency. They are overseen by no legislature, accountable to no courts. No citizen can sue them for nonperformance of duty. They answer to no freedom-of-information act or other effective rules of transparency. Experiences recounted by UN employees are strangely mixed. Some tell of lucrative sinecures, while others tell of mistreatment without recourse to any labor laws. Little wonder that the scores on the staff survey for "integrity" and "trust" were so low (see p. 49).

When Kofi Annan overruled the UN's own investigative unit, OIOS, and exonerated the High Commissioner for Refugees of sexual harassment, he offered no substantive explanation, and he ordered that the OIOS report that detailed the commissioner's guilt be kept secret. When America was voted down for a seat at the 2002 meeting of the Human Rights Commission, U.S. diplomats expressed consternation because enough votes had been pledged to them privately to win.[7] Obviously, some of those who had given pledges had gone back on them. But why not? The ballot is secret, an incomprehensible procedure when states are the electors rather than citizens.

In this shrouded environment, cynical deals are common. The member-states are more inclined to scratch each other's backs than to suffer diplomatic friction over matters of mere principle. A key reason for the execrable record of the Commission on Human Rights was pointed out in the 2004 report of the High-Level Panel on Threats, Challenges, and Change. "In recent years States have sought membership of the Commission not to strengthen human rights but to protect themselves against criticism or to criticize others," it said.[8]

This is true, but what the panel did not go on to address was how it is that states who seek commission seats for such base reasons succeed in getting them. Members on the Commission are elected by the Economic and Social Council. Why do other states vote to elect abusive governments? The simple answer is horse-trading. A seat on the Commission is often more valuable to an abusive government that wants to shield itself than to others (who might prefer, instead, a seat on one of the agencies that can influence the dispensing of material resources). So votes are exchanged. These others may be democracies, but not all democracies are above such barter.

Nor is the Commission on Human Rights the only body to which inappropriate members get elected. This happens even with the Security Council, whose nonpermanent members are elected by the General Assembly. In 2002, Syria was elected to one of these seats. But at the time, an estimated twenty thousand Syrian troops and intelligence agents occupied Lebanon, robbing it of meaningful sovereignty; for nearly thirty years, Lebanon's political life had been dictated from Damascus. A Security Council resolution adopted in 1982 demanded "strict respect for the sovereignty . . . and political independence of Lebanon."[9] But Syria's utter disregard for this resolution not only went unpenalized; it did not prevent Syria's election to the council. If defiance of Security Council resolutions is not grounds even for disqualification from the council itself, what possible pressure is there to take the resolutions seriously?

Serving Its Own Interests

Confronted with the litany of the UN's failures, its defenders are wont to say that it is not the UN that is to blame but the member-states, for the UN is nothing more than the sum of its members. This is a facile excuse. Although the champions of the UN usually also present themselves as devotees of international law, this argument ignores the law, since it is long established that the UN has legal "personality" in its own right. The International Court of Justice ruled in 1949 that, legally, the UN "is an international person . . . it is a subject of international law and capable of possessing international rights and duties."[10]

This "personality" is not merely a legal conceit. Any organization the size of the UN takes on a life of its own. The UN's budget—including all the costs of peacekeeping operations—is larger than those of two-thirds of the world's countries. According to chapter XV, article 99 of the UN charter, the secretary general is endowed with authority to "bring to the attention of the Security Council any matter which in his opinion may threaten the maintenance of international peace and security," just as a member-state may do. He frequently appoints special representatives who play significant roles in international crises. And he may even take on such a role himself, such as when Kofi Annan flew off to Baghdad in 1998 to forestall U.S. bombing.

Unsurprisingly, the officers and the staff of the UN are often devoted strongly to the institution's own interests. A clear sense of this gelled as early as the 1960–64 crisis in the Congo, the UN's first ambitious intervention in a civil war. A multisided hornets' nest of a civil war, it cost the life of Secretary General Dag Hammerskjöld, and still no satisfactory outcome was achieved, leaving the organization with diminished credibility in an era before much of the world had grown jaded about it. UN staff seemed to feel the wound to their own organization more keenly than they did the sad fate of the Congo, and were determined to avoid such exposure in the future. Righter observes, "The moral that many UN officials drew was that the UN's prestige mattered more than its effectiveness."[11]

This mindset remained with the body ever after, revealing itself most devastatingly thirty years later when hell broke loose in Rwanda. Michael Barnett has described how the first impulse of UN officials was to protect the organization. Boutros-Ghali kept to himself and his top deputies the appalling information he was receiving from General Dallaire, apparently because he did not want the UN to get itself into a thicket.[12] This self-serving response was not limited to staff. Barnett observed much the same spirit in the Security Council. "The council's debate gave priority to the threat to the peacekeepers and the future of the UN. What was at stake was bigger than Rwanda," he reports.[13] Boutros-Ghali set the tone, but there was little dissent from the members.

Similarly, the members of NAM are highly invested in the interests of the UN as such. This is not a matter of idealism so much as self-interest. The greatest leverage that many small, weak states possess in international politics is their seat in the UN, one arena in which they stand equal with mightier and richer states. Righter reports: "Because the strategy of confrontation depended, critically, on the authority commanded by the United Nations and its place in international decision making, 'strengthening' the UN became an obsession with the nonaligned. It figured on the agenda of every summit."[14]

Member-states and UN officials alike take for granted that the organization has a role of its own in various top-priority crises and issues. Who has challenged the composition of the so-called quartet of mediators of the Israeli-Palestinian conflict? It consists of the United States, Russia, the European Union, and the UN. No one has said that since the UN is nothing but the cumulation of the other three quartet members, plus some other states, it makes no sense for it to be a party. Rather, it is acknowledged that the UN is a "player" in Middle East diplomacy in its own right. Likewise in Bosnia, the secretary general and his representatives insisted on a "dual-key" constraint on the use of air power against forces that were breaking the peace. This required the consent both of NATO, which would carry out any bombardment, and of the representative of the UN secretariat.

The point that the UN's failures ought properly to be laid at the doorsteps of the member-states is not new. Years before the UN was born, Winston Churchill defended the League of Nations on similar grounds: "It was wrong to say that the League had failed. It was rather the member states who had failed the League."[15] Perhaps this is so, but it begs the inference that there is something about such organizations as the League and the UN that encourages states to behave fecklessly or irresponsibly. The obstacle of the Security Council provided a convenient pretext for the United States to avoid taking any forceful action in Bosnia at a time when President Clinton wanted to focus on domestic issues and avoid being drawn into the Balkans. Several nations exhibited pangs of conscience during the Rwanda genocide in 1994, but Washington's insistence on blocking any action in the Security Council let them off the hook. In 2005, the threat of a Chinese veto inhibited an adequate response to ethnic cleansing in Darfur, offering a comfortable excuse to Western states reluctant to become directly involved.

The nature of the institution seems to invite evasion and procrastination rather than moral seriousness and resolute action. Churchill implied as much when he argued for constructing international organizations in the wake of World War II along regional rather than global lines. Whatever the cause, it is hard to see the justification for organizations if they call forth not the best in the member-states, but rather the most equivocal and pusillanimous.

5

Proposals for Reform:
Hope Springs Eternal

In November 2004, the High-Level Panel on Threats, Challenges, and Change presented its comprehensive plan for revising the UN, including 101 specific recommendations.[1] This was followed in March 2005 by the issuance of an even broader report by Secretary General Annan. Entitled *In Larger Freedom: Towards Development, Security, and Human Rights for All,* it embraces and amends the proposals of the High-Level Panel while also dealing with a range of economic and social issues flowing from the UN's September 2000 Millennium Summit.[2]

These two weighty documents are only the latest of many reform initiatives since Annan acceded to the post of secretary general. In 2003, the UN received the recommendations of the Panel of Eminent Persons on United Nations–Civil Society Relations[3] that Annan had appointed, and in his recent report he reaffirmed his endorsement of those recommendations. This, in turn, followed the secretary general's 2002 program of reform[4] and the Millennium Summit, which issued the *Millennium Report*, dealing in part with UN reform.[5] This was preceded by the 1997 program for reform proposed by Annan and adopted by the General Assembly in December that year.[6]

If Secretary General Annan seems to have paid considerable attention to the issue of reform, his predecessors were concerned with it as well. In 1993 Boutros-Ghali had sponsored the creation of an Independent Working Group on the Future of the United Nations, funded by the Ford Foundation. No sooner had this group issued its report in May 1995 than Boutros-Ghali appointed another such body, the Commission on Global Governance. And before Boutros-Ghali, there were other attempts at reform. Righter points out that a 1993 General Assembly resolution on "Restructuring and Revitalization of the United Nations in the Economic, Social and Related Fields" starts, in the fashion of UN resolutions, by citing fifteen previous such resolutions stretching back to 1946.[7]

Professor Edward Luck, former head of the United Nations Association, notes that back in 1945, "before the UN could hold its first meeting, a number of states were already calling for its reform." Luck sees this long history as a sign of strength. "Does the deja vu nature of UN reform suggest that nothing changes or that reform is bound to fail?" he asks, then answers:

> Not at all; indeed it could be argued that change is one of the few constants in the UN system. It incessantly has to adapt to an evolving mosaic of demands, priorities, and initiatives on the part of the Member States and public constituencies. . . . And few institutions are so fond of producing or co-opting fresh conceptual and doctrinal approaches to addressing the world's problems.[8]

Luck's reply to his own rhetorical question is intended to be reassuring, but it has quite the reverse effect. For all the reform, adaptation, and fresh approaches, the UN does not function better today than at its founding. In some ways it functions worse. As Righter observed, "Fat reams of reform blueprints moulder in [UN] archives. All, good or bad, were given a ceremonial welcome, then sabotaged or hacked to pieces. None secured the termination of a single useless activity."[9] This stubborn reality suggests that the organization is impervious to useful reform.

Both the report of the High-Level Panel and Annan's *In Larger Freedom* address issues of UN reform, as well as loftier questions about the mission, performance, and legitimacy of the UN. Let us consider the reform issues before turning to the others. Jeffrey Laurenti of the UN Foundation has offered a useful taxonomy of UN reform proposals. They fall into three categories, he says: improving the UN's efficiency, enhancing its capabilities, and revising its political structures.[10]

Improving the UN's Efficiency

The quest for greater efficiency for the UN has a long pedigree. In 1993, former U.S. attorney general Dick Thornburgh completed a year's stint as undersecretary general for administration and management of the UN (a post that often goes to an American), and wrote a scathing report on the state of UN administration. He found that the organization was "burdened with an inordinate number of supernumeraries—those serving in high-paying permanent contracts without any specific job assignment"; that its budget process was "almost surreal" insofar as a great share of its expenditures was not in the "budget"; and that it was "totally lacking in effective means to deal with fraud, waste and abuse by staff members."[11] The specific remedies that Thornburgh proposed went up in flames, literally, as Boutros-Ghali boasted that he burned the undersecretary general's report.

Nonetheless, Boutros-Ghali did embrace the cause of management reform, ordering the elimination of a number of positions. But the perception that he was insufficiently dedicated to this mission fueled the U.S. decision to oppose his reelection.

His successor, Kofi Annan, attacked the problem more vigorously. Annan's 1997 and 2002 reform programs comprise altogether more than one hundred fifty specific measures, mostly aimed at improving efficiency. But whether they will produce a streamlined UN or merely serve to blanket the organization's critics in a blizzard of detail is unclear. The U.S. General Accounting Office assessed the progress in 2004 and determined that 60 percent of the eighty-eight specific initiatives of 1997 and 38 percent of the sixty-six initiatives of 2002 had been implemented, but even the GAO could not compute what this all added up to. Its report concluded:

We identified several challenges that may impact the Secretariat's ability to meet the overall goals of the reforms. First, the Secretariat does not conduct periodic, comprehensive assessments of the status and impact of reforms. Without such assessments, the Secretariat cannot determine if it is meeting the Secretary General's overall reform goals or identify areas where further improvements are needed. Second, the 2002 reform agenda did not differentiate between short- and long-term goals. Setting implementation goals and a timeline is a key practice for organizations engaged in change management initiatives. Third, some managers have resisted implementing certain reforms, but their support is critical for the institutionalization of reforms in the long term. Fourth, several U.N. officials we spoke with stated that reforms were delayed because additional resources were not made available for their implementation. The Secretary General stated that departments would need to implement reforms within existing resources because additional funding would not be available in the regular budget.[12]

In presenting their report in 2004, members of the High-Level Panel said they had been told that "deadwood" was still an important obstacle to the UN's efficient operation, and their report proposed a "one-time" buyout to pension it off. At the same time, in contrast to previous reform proposals that had found the organization overstaffed, the report proposed giving the secretary general an additional sixty positions, as well as another deputy secretary general. The secretary general endorsed the idea of a buyout, "so as to refresh and realign the staff to meet current needs," but instead of another deputy, he asked to be given "a higher level of managerial authority and flexibility [including] the ability to adjust the staffing table as necessary and without undue constraint."[13]

It is hard to see how a buyout will solve anything. Neither the panel nor the secretary general addressed the question of where the deadwood came from. The obvious answer is that it is the fruit of distributing jobs by nationality rather than by qualification. In his report, Annan went out of his way to reaffirm the traditional distribution of jobs by geography, with the fillip, "We must add today, ensuring a just balance between men and women." In short, he proposes to make what was already the world's most baroque system of affirmative action even more complex and demanding. The result is predictable: deadwood will be bought out and replaced by new deadwood.

The most noteworthy improvement in efficiency of recent years stemmed not from a reform program but rather from the withholding of U.S. dues to the UN on the orders of Congress.[14] The so-called Helms-Biden bill demanded a reduction in Washington's share of the total UN dues assessment. A compromise resolution of this dispute led to restraint of the growth of the UN's central budget (not including peacekeeping operations), which was held constant for several years. It also resulted in an important reform in how the budgets are adopted. Previously this was done by a simple majority, which meant that states that paid minimal dues could enact budget increases, the costs of which would have to be shouldered by the wealthy few, first and foremost the United States. To be sure, the U.S. goal in changing this system was selfish, but the budgetary discipline imposed was a welcome change.

In addition to changing the hiring and budgetary systems, the most important way in which the UN's administrative performance could be improved would be to tear away the cloak of secrecy that shrouds so much of its operation. When the oil-for-food scandal broke, the fact that there had been fifty-five internal audits that had been kept from the member-states was a source of embarrassment. The General Assembly passed a resolution changing this practice. In his report, Annan claims he is opening things further: "I am in the process of identifying other categories of information that could be made available routinely."[15]

But how much transparency is achieved if it is left to the head of an organization to determine what it shall reveal? The cause of UN reform would be far better served by the implementation of something along the lines of the Freedom of Information Act, making all information publicly available except such items as the officials can show would be harmful to reveal.

Enhancing the UN's Capabilities

The second of Laurenti's categories, reforms that would enhance the UN's capabilities, has, at least for the last decade, been occupied mostly by the issue of peacekeeping. The sudden explosion in the number of peacekeeping missions in the aftermath of the Cold War found the institution woefully unprepared. Michael Barnett describes what he found when he arrived at the UN:

> Until 1993 there was no "situation room," with the very dire implication that if a field commander got into trouble over the weekend, there literally was no one to reach at the UN headquarters in New York. As UN Protection Force (UNPROFOR) Commander Lewis McKenzie once controversially exclaimed, "If you are a commander of a UN mission, don't get in trouble after five P.M. or on the weekend. There is no one in the UN to answer the phone!" Soon after that statement was made, the UN created a situation room. Compared to the situation rooms in most states, it was almost comically outfitted: 1950s fake wood paneling, makeshift maps on the wall, an array of phones sitting on top of mismatched desks, and a few, scattered fax machines. It looked more like the accommodations for a public-access television station than it did the military nerve center for very tenuous peacekeeping operations.[16]

After the acknowledged peacekeeping disasters of Bosnia, Somalia, and Rwanda in the 1990s, the organization moved both to restrain its involvement in peacekeeping and to improve its capacity. Various piecemeal changes were attempted in the late 1990s, and then in 2000 a Panel on United Nations Peace Operations chaired by Lakhdar Brahimi offered more comprehensive proposals for improving UN peacekeeping. It recommended an overhaul of the management and budget of these missions, creation of logistical facilities for rapid deployments, assembly of standby lists of military and police personnel qualified and available for UN missions, a new doctrine including "robust rules of engagement," and countless bureaucratic changes.[17]

Unfortunately, as Lord David Hannay, former UK ambassador to the UN and a member of the High-Level Panel reported, "The Brahimi report, which contained much excellent advice and recommendations, was only partially implemented. The member states were ready to will the ends but not the means to achieve them."[18] One advance has been that UN missions in such places as the Congo have adopted more aggressive rules of engagement.[19] Still, the UN is far from being able to impose peace in nonpermissive settings.

The High-Level Panel did not have much to say about augmenting peacekeeping capabilities, except that the new deputy secretary general position that it recommended would apparently have this in its portfolio. It did, however, propose to enhance UN capabilities in two other ways. One was by creating a "Peacebuilding Commission" that would "identify countries that are under stress and risk sliding toward State collapse" in order to "prevent that process from developing further."[20] This begs the question of how such prevention would be achieved. In Yugoslavia, for example, everyone saw the "slide," and frantic diplomatic efforts were extended—to no particular effect. The Peacebuilding Commission would also be charged with mobilizing resources to help fragile governments get on their feet in the wake of conflicts.[21] Annan's report endorsed the idea of a Peacebuilding Commission (and also a Peacebuilding Support Office within the secretariat), but it focused exclusively on the second of the above tasks—aiding in recovery from conflict—which is clearly the more doable.

Wisely, Annan did not take up the other of the High-Level Panel's proposed enhancements in this field, namely the creation of a Committee on the Social and Economic Aspects of Security

Threats that would "commission research and develop better understanding about the economic and social threats to peace, and about the economic and social aspects of other threats, such as terrorism and organized crime."[22] This all sounds less like a reform than an antireform, a mandate to spend money for a hopelessly vague purpose through research, which is an endeavor that the UN is not designed for.

One other way in which some believe the UN's capacities might be enhanced is by reaching out to nongovernmental forces. This was the apparent thought behind Annan's other recent reform exercise, the Panel of Eminent Persons on UN–Civil Society Relations, whose report he reaffirmed in his 2005 report. The thrust of this initiative, however, remains murky, thanks in part to the panel's penchant for jargon. It began, for example, by recommending that the UN "foster . . . multi-constituency processes" through "multistakeholder partnerships," recognizing that "the key actors are different for different issues," whatever all that may mean.[23]

The term "civil society" was brought into the lexicon by dissidents within the Soviet bloc in the 1980s. If the UN's sudden interest in this concept means that it will be less beholden to dictatorial governments in favor of their oppressed subjects, it would be a major reform indeed. It might mean, for example, that the Commission on Human Rights could finally perform the mission that its name suggests. But it is difficult to imagine that such a welcome change would be accomplished. Nor does not it seem that this is what Annan and the Eminent Persons have in mind.

Rather, the panel's report focuses on defects of democracy. These are to be found in democracy's inadequate relationship to "global governance." "Concerning democracy," says the report,

> a clear paradox is emerging: while the substance of politics is fast globalizing (in the areas of trade, economics, environment, pandemics, terrorism, etc.), the process of politics is not; its principal institutions (elections, political parties and parliaments) remain firmly rooted at the national or local level.[24]

It goes on to say that modern technology makes it possible to over-come this weakness by allowing citizens to participate in global governance through "civil society."

While none too clear, this seems to point in the direction of strengthening multilateral institutions through direct links to citi-zens, unmediated by their governments. It is, in other words, a method of vitiating national sovereignty. To batter the ramparts of sovereignty of highly authoritarian regimes is one thing. But to focus, as the Eminent Persons seem to do, on the sovereignty of democracies is troubling. One recent example of a UN exercise in global governance that came to be shaped in large part by NGOs, the embodiment of civil society, was the 2001 World Conference Against Racism in Durban, which degenerated into a kind of lynch mob—scarcely an encouraging precedent.

Revising the UN's Political Structures

Reforms of the political structure of the UN have traditionally focused on changing the functioning of the Security Council, either by enlarging it or by eliminating or reducing the veto power of its five permanent members. However, the High-Level Panel and the secretary general have put some other issues on the table. They acknowledge that the General Assembly has lost respect:

> Its norm-making capacity is often squandered on debates about minutiae or thematic topics outpaced by real-world events. Its inability to reach closure on issues undermines its relevance. An unwieldy and static agenda leads to repetitive debates.[25]

But the only remedies the panel can offer are unimpressive: "better conceptualization and shortening of the agenda" and "smaller, more tightly focused committees."[26] Annan's report offers much the same pabulum, but spices it up by calling it these "bold measures."[27]

However dysfunctional the General Assembly, the condition of the Commission on Human Rights is even worse. The panel damned the CHR, saying it "suffers from a legitimacy deficit that casts doubt on the overall reputation of the United Nations."[28] Annan, as we have seen, confessed much the same. But what can be done about it?

The panel proposed to replace the commission with one on which every one of the UN's members would sit, just as in the General Assembly. Indeed, it would in effect be the General Assembly in special session. Given what the panel found about the performance of the assembly, however, this does not sound like a promising solution. Annan's proposal is to rename the body a council rather than a commission, and have it elected by two-thirds vote of the General Assembly. The theory is that it will be harder for the worst violators of human rights to win two-thirds. But it is far from certain that this would be true. Those same states have normally secured their seats by consensus, not by narrow majorities.

Annan also called for transformation of the governance of the World Bank and the International Monetary Fund (IMF), in order to "broaden and strengthen the participation of developing and transition countries in international economic decision-making and norm-setting" and "to overcome the widespread perception among developing countries that they are underrepresented in both bodies."[29] Developing countries are not, of course, underrepresented as beneficiaries of these institutions, to which the rich countries donate funds to benefit the poor. However, since voting in these bodies is based on the amount of each country's financial contribution, the givers have more weight than the receivers. This may well be the reason why, by most accounts, these financial institutions have functioned at a higher level of efficiency, integrity, and accomplishment than the UN. Annan, himself, confessed that there is "declining public confidence in the United Nations";[30] no one says the like about the World Bank or IMF.

As for the Security Council, the panel mooted two approaches, without expressing preference for one over the other, and Annan followed its lead. Either approach would raise the number of members of the council from fifteen to twenty-four including, in one case, six new permanent memberships or, in the other, eight new seats of renewable four-year tenure. Neither would give any of the new members a veto.

One constant of these and other proposals to enlarge the Security Council is that inevitably they would make the council more unwieldy and dilute the power of the United States. It is hard to imagine that this would be in America's interests, but it might not be in anyone else's, either. Without a veto, the Security Council acts by majority (or, rather, supermajority; nine votes out of fifteen are required to pass a motion), but it attempts to find consensus. Its deliberations will surely be less fruitful if it expands by sixty percent.

One of the reasons for change, said the panel, is that "the distribution of power among members has changed."[31] As the panel notes, the UN framers sought to strike a balance between idealism and reality. The idealistic notion of the equality of states was honored in the design of the General Assembly, in which each nation has as much voice and vote as any other. But the reality of unequal power was acknowledged in the design of the Security Council. The framers thought it essential to take this situation into account, believing that if the structure of the UN diverged too far from the "facts on the ground" it would become a paper body. By such reasoning, the composition of the council should evolve to reflect changing circumstances. As Annan put it, "The Security Council must be broadly representative of the realities of power in today's world."[32] Therefore, the panel urged adjustments to take into account the growing economic, demographic, or political weight of two key groups of states that had been left out of the original design: the losers of World War II and the former colonies.

Are Britain, France, Russia, and China more important than Germany, Japan, or India? They are not, and the logic of trying to remedy this is hard to gainsay. But the panel took no note of the most important discrepancy between the configuration of the council and the realities of world power. It is not the absence of one or another country from among the permanent members. Rather, it is the equating of the other four permanent members with the United States, when the burdens of defending the peace fall so overwhelmingly on America.

Various other reform proposals have been advanced by private groups or scholars. The most important one—embodied in a report of a 2002 joint task force of the Council of Foreign Relations and Freedom House—urges the formation of a "democracy caucus" within the UN.[33] Formally speaking, this is not a reform, since it does not entail amending the organization's rules or reshaping its bodies. If such a caucus could be formed, and if its members allowed themselves to be influenced by it in their voting patterns within the UN, this would surely be a step forward. Although it might not make much difference in the organization's presumptive core function of keeping the peace, it could ensure a different composition of the membership of the Commission on Human Rights, and to that degree it might serve to reclaim some of the UN's moral stature. Such a caucus might comprise a majority of the UN membership. If it were unified it could supplant the Non-Aligned Movement as the organization's dominant faction, and change the tone of the General Assembly and much else.

It is, however, uncertain that the democracies would cooperate. Countries like Poland and the Czech Republic, still in the flush of democracy's triumph and eager to remain close to the United States, can be counted on to take part. But others may see such a caucus as a means of enhancing American leverage, and for many governments—including democratic ones—the resentment of U.S. power is a stronger feeling than any spirit of solidarity with fellow democracies. Western Europeans are busy forging a tighter European Union largely for the motive of counterbalancing America. As the EU struggles to make a common defense and security policy a reality, it is doubtful that its members will have political energy for a closer merging of all democracies.

Nor is it likely that most third-world democracies will put democratic identity ahead of their regional or "nonaligned" identity. In the General Assembly in recent years, the other industrialized democracies have voted in line with the United States most of the time. But democracies in the developing countries vote in closer correlation with the dictatorships of their regions.[34] Illustratively, few nations have historically voted as antithetically to the United States as has India, the longest-standing democracy in the Third World, but also a proud leader of the Non-Aligned Movement. In the year 2000, for example, India ranked 169th out of 188 other UN members in terms of voting correspondence with the United States in the General Assembly. In other words, it was at odds with us more often than such hostile states as Iran, Libya, or Afghanistan under the Taliban; more often, too, than such tyrannies as Burma, Vietnam, and Saudi Arabia.

Since the attacks on America of September 11, 2001, the common threat of radical Islamic terrorism has brought India and the United States closer, and India's rank has risen appreciably in voting correspondence with the United States. But even so, in 2004, India voted contrary to the United States 80 percent of the time in the General Assembly (not including consensus decisions). A nation like India might calculate that it wields more influence as a leader of the NAM than it would in a democracy caucus that would likely be dominated by Washington.

On the other hand, such a calculation might prove wrong; Washington might not dominate. There is a possibility that a democracy caucus could backfire on the United States in an era when U.S. policies are unpopular abroad, even in democratic countries. This seems a risk worth taking; but a combine of democracies is likely to work better as a freestanding entity than within the doleful atmosphere of the UN.

More important by far than any of the specific reforms proposed by the High-Level Panel is the argument it puts forth about the past and future of the UN and its relation to the United States. "We found," says the panel, "that the United Nations has been much more effective in addressing the major threats to peace and security than it is given credit for."[35] It argues that there were far fewer wars in the second half of the twentieth century than would have been expected by historical extrapolation, and that this is owing in part to the UN:

The United Nations diminished the threat of inter-state war in several ways. Peace was furthered by the invention of peacekeeping; diplomacy was carried out by the Secretary-General; disputes were remedied under the International Court of Justice; and a strong norm was upheld against aggressive war.[36]

It was not only interstate war that was prevented, says the panel. "Since 1992, civil wars have declined steadily. . . . In the last 15 years, more civil wars were ended through negotiation than in the previous two centuries—in large part because the United Nations provided leadership, opportunities for negotiation, strategic coordination, and the resources needed for implementation," the report avers.[37]

In view of this proud record, the panel finds itself well satisfied with the existing institutional arrangements. "The Charter as a whole continues to provide a sound legal and policy basis for the organization of collective security, enabling the Security Council to respond to threats to international peace and security, both old and new, in a timely and effective manner."[38] The allusion to new threats refers to the issue raised by President Bush in his September 2002 National Security Strategy, namely that weapons of mass destruction in the hands of terrorists or lawless regimes can justify preemptive action. (Some critics of Bush's argument say that the proper term for what he proposes is "preventive" action rather than "preemptive," reserving the latter term for situations of imminent attack.)[39]

The panel concedes that such a threat is imaginable and might require a military response. However, it firmly repudiates any expansion of the article of the charter (article 51) that recognizes the right of self-defense. As currently written, that article refers only to the situation when "an armed attack occurs." But what if a state has reason to believe that such a fatal attack is in train? "The short answer," says the panel, "is that if there are good arguments for preventive military action, with good evidence to support them, they should be put to the Security Council, which can authorize such action if it chooses to."[40] Annan's report takes a like approach.[41]

Both reports are at pains to secure and extend the authority of the Security Council. On the one hand, this applies to situations of gross human rights abuse. Although the charter proclaims a strict observance of national sovereignty, forswearing the authority "to intervene in matters which are essentially within the domestic jurisdiction of any state," both reports note approvingly the growing acceptance of lifesaving intervention. And, in terms explicitly endorsed by Annan, the panel attempts to codify this by asserting that

> history teaches us all too clearly that it cannot be assumed that every State will always be able, or willing, to meet its responsibilities to protect its own people. And in those circumstances, the principles of collective security mean that some portion of those responsibilities should be taken up by the international community.[42]

The Security Council and the United States

The bigger questions about the Security Council's authority, however, do not concern humanitarian intervention, but rather the council's relationship to the United States. This issue reached a boil in the debate over the Iraq war and was, in fact, what precipitated the creation of the High-Level Panel. The panel, it should come as no surprise, comes down squarely against any American infringements. "The yearning for an international system governed by the rule of law has grown," it says, noting that, conversely, "there is little evident international acceptance of the idea of security being best preserved by . . . any single—even benignly motivated—superpower."[43] Vigilant against any possibility that Washington will attempt an end-run around the council's authority, the panel goes out of its way to mention NATO's recent "out-of-area" missions (such as in Afghanistan): "We welcome this so long as these operations are authorized by and accountable to the Security Council."[44]

For his part, Annan goes even further in trying to clip America's wings. His report cites the "key challenges" that have arisen in the twenty-first century. The first is the terror attacks of 9/11, and the second is this: "Many States have begun to feel that the sheer imbalance of power in the world is a source of instability."[45]

He is alluding, of course, to American supremacy. Apparently, in his view, the world faces a dual menace: al Qaeda and the United States. Accordingly, the report is sprinkled with allusions to treaties that Washington eschews, for example, calling on "member States to cooperate fully with the International Criminal Court," an implicit appeal not to sign bilateral treaties with the United States, as many have done, that promise not to deliver American soldiers to this court to which America is not a party.[46]

Annan also declaims that "support for the rule of law must be strengthened by universal participation in multilateral conventions," some of which the United States does not participate in.[47] This is an effort to shift the rules of the game. International law is on the whole voluntary, consisting mainly of treaties freely entered into. The measure of rule of law has always been the degree to which states uphold the treaties they sign, not any obligation to sign treaties they find unwise. To assert the latter standard is to offer a new and less voluntary conception of the law. Whether this would serve the interests of America or of justice is an open question.

Although Annan does a service by throwing his weight behind the commonsense definition of terrorism that the UN has for so long resisted (namely, that it is defined by the nature of the act, not the purpose for which it is carried out), his report warned that in battling terrorism, "we must never compromise human rights" for fear of "ceding the moral high ground."[48]

Perhaps this alludes to Middle Eastern dictatorships that have fought terrorists with rough methods, but human rights are violated routinely in these countries, terrorism or no. Annan's injunction seems to be aimed more at the American war against terrorism. In that case, in view of the historical record, it is nonsense. Arguably the greatest victories for human rights in history were the American-led victory over the Axis in World War II and the American-led victory over Soviet communism in the Cold War. In both of these wars, human rights were "compromised." And, one might add, the greatest victory for human rights in America's history was the North's victory in the Civil War, in the course of which President Lincoln suspended the right of habeas corpus.

In short, human rights are often compromised in wars in which defense of human rights is one of the purposes. To compound his nonsense, Annan proposed "to create a special rapporteur who would report to the Commission on Human Rights on the compatibility on counter-terrorism measures with international human rights laws."[49] In other words, he would create an investigation into U.S. practices, and the investigator would report back to the selfsame "human rights" commission that includes the likes of China, Cuba, Sudan, Libya, and Saudi Arabia—the same commission that he himself has complained "casts a shadow on the reputation of the UN as a whole."[50]

Right or wrong in its treatment of peace and security, what is perhaps most striking is their secondary or even tertiary status in the secretary general's report, even though these were the central purposes for which the UN was founded. Neither did it give pride of place to matters of UN reform, despite the fact that the organization was in the midst of the most damaging scandal in its history. Rather, the principal focus of Annan's report was the problem of poverty. It might cogently be argued that the deprivation suffered by many millions is far more important than the misdeeds of a few. But the way Annan melded his report gave the feeling that he was, above all, trying to change the subject away from the misdeeds of his subordinates and family members and his own misjudgments.

Moreover, it is hard to make a case that the UN is an effective agency for alleviating the suffering. As noted previously, the world body has a sad record of propounding economic nostrums that perpetuated or worsened poverty rather than alleviating it. These nostrums were rooted in the spirit of third-world resentment toward the West and in a belief in the efficacy of the state as an economic agency.

Despite bows in the direction of private enterprise, Annan's report is redolent of this spirit and this belief. It is filled with heroic blather reminiscent of Mao Zedong ("Only by acting decisively . . . can we . . . win a decisive victory")[51] and veiled threats ("We will not enjoy security without development"),[52] and rhetoric that is bloviated and self-congratulatory:

> The multifaceted challenge of development cuts across a vast array of interlinked issues—ranging from gender equality through health and education to the environment. The historic United Nations conferences and summits held in the 1990s helped build a comprehensive normative framework around these linkages for the first time by mapping out a broad vision of shared development priorities.[53]

To give all this an aura of accomplishment, numeric goals and dates are arbitrarily attached, above all to halve world poverty by 2015, which resemble nothing so much as that tired relic of twentieth-century dystopia—the five-year plan.

6

A Better Approach

The contributions of the High-Level Panel and secretary general in defining terrorism, codifying the limitations on sovereignty, and in some other areas are valuable. But on the question at the heart of the UN's purpose—how to keep the peace—they would lead us in the wrong direction. The errors begin with delusions about the UN's record. The panel claims that the UN has contributed substantially to keeping the peace, but it offers few examples. It offers lists of ways in which the UN has allegedly helped—for example, it says that the secretary general has conducted diplomacy—but it does not tell us where that forestalled a war. In the voice of the panel, the UN is like the proverbial rooster who believes that his crowing makes the sun rise.

Yes, there has been a sharp decrease in interstate war. But does the credit for this belong to the UN or to the United States? Surely, what preserved the peace of Europe after World War II was the Marshall Plan, the political transformation of (West) Germany engineered by the American-led occupation, America's military power embedded in NATO, and the commitment to face down a Russian Communist regime that had already gobbled up dozens of its neighbors and was eager to swallow more. America's alliances with Japan, Australia, South Korea, and Taiwan have, to a large extent, kept peace in Asia. American intervention prevented Iraq from conquering the Persian Gulf in 1990 and deterred Syria from attacking Jordan in 1970. In Latin America, which has been mostly calm for reasons having little to do with the United States, America has suppressed and constrained radical guerrillas who have sought to roil the waters. Moreover, the decrease in civil wars adduced by the panel is owing to the same cause—America's victory in the Cold War. The peaceful resolution of internecine conflicts in Central America, Southern Africa, and elsewhere, including most of the list of places where UN peacekeeping succeeded, flowed directly from that triumph.

The role of America in fostering peace is larger than the sum of these parts. America's supremacy is probably unprecedented. What is surely unprecedented is for a single power to be at once dominant and so little inclined to conquest. Some speak loosely of an American "empire." But if America has an empire, it is unlike any other, for the United States has in modern times taken no other territories as its own, and it governs none. Nor can anyone say what are the borders of this "empire." True, America exerts influence all over the world and sometimes asserts its will by military means where others think it should not. But all of this activity is in pursuit of what the political scientist Arnold Wolfers called "milieu goals" as opposed to "possession goals."[1] Acting from enlightened self-interest, it seeks to encourage (and occasionally to impose) an order that is lawful, democratic, and prosperous.

In other eras, the strongest powers were more self-aggrandizing, and this made for wars. But there is an additional reason why America's power has helped make the world more peaceful today. Because of its stance for world peace and order, however inconsistently applied, every would-be aggressor must calculate America's likely response. From Saddam Hussein to Slobodan Milosevic to Adolf Hitler, many of their ilk have come to bad ends. There is no way of counting how many others have been deterred.

Recognition of this reality would lead to a very different approach to reforming the Security Council. The panel says that a key reason for change is to bring the composition of the council into accord with today's realities, but it offers no remedy for the chief incongruity, namely, the failure to reflect the reality of America's disproportionate power. That disparity in power is reflected in one way in the Security Council: dues assessments. The U.S. assessment constitutes 22 percent of the UN's operating budget (which reflects a reduction after a bitter and prolonged quarrel instigated by

Congress). The combined assessments of the other four permanent members of the council equal just over 17 percent.

More important than the mere fact of power is the willingness of the United States to use its power to uphold the peace. That this power is not only essential but also benign is evidenced by the fact that in neither Europe nor Asia do most countries wish to see the departure of America's tangible military presence. More to the point, the two times in the UN's history when it has taken forceful action to counteract an international breach of the peace—in Korea and Kuwait—it turned to the United States to take action under article 51 rather than making even the pretense of activating its own putative peace-enforcement machinery.

The unique burden the United States bears of being, in effect, the Security Council's sword should be reflected in the council's decision-making structure. One way to achieve this would be to change the status of the other four currently permanent members. It is anomalous that they are placed on a plane with the United States rather than with the other secondary powers. What sense does it make that France is a permanent member while Germany is not? That China is a member but Japan is not? Russia but not India? No one has dared propose removing these other four permanent members from their seats, but why should they each have a veto? A restructuring that would end some of the anomalies of the current system would increase the number of permanent members but change the veto system. Only the United States would retain the power to veto a motion by its own vote. The other permanent members could also exercise a veto, but only, say, if three of them joined together

The UN would benefit from a more fundamental overhaul than tinkering with the composition of the Security Council. Timothy Wirth of the UN Foundation likes to draw a distinction between the political bodies which, he says, absorb only 20 percent of the organization's budget and which, he acknowledges, are hard to defend; and the specialized agencies—the World Health Organization, UNICEF, the High Commissioner for Refugees and the like—that perform the organization's valuable humanitarian work.[2] This dichotomy suggests a kind of radical surgery that might return the UN to health. After sixty years, isn't it time to recognize that the political UN is a failure? Why not abolish altogether the General Assembly and the Security Council, along with other useless or pernicious agencies, like the Commission on Human Rights and the various special bodies devoted to the Palestinian struggle?

The point is not to abolish the UN but to liberalize it, so that the diplomatic analog of a free market might flourish. Neither is the point to separate the United States from the other nations, but to allow discourse and cooperation freed from the straitjacket of bodies that serve no demonstrated purpose. Americans, following the liberal philosophers, believe that government is a necessary evil. World government, however, is an unnecessary evil. The effort to be a proto–world government is the crux of the UN's worst failings.

The world needs communication among states, and, yes, it needs multilateral action. But it does not need artificial structures any more than an economy needs a jungle of regulations. In its political function, the UN ought simply to be a center for multilateral diplomacy. Nations could talk and agree to do whatever they agreed to do, free from the distortions introduced by the spurious solemnity of the General Assembly or the paralyzing requirement of Security Council consensus. Meanwhile, the valuable humanitarian agencies could go about their tasks with fewer noisome political pressures.

This approach would make it possible to reduce radically the UN secretariat to an essentially administrative function. It might be able to get by on a small fraction of its current staff and budget, and the savings could be devoted to the humanitarian work.

It would still leave in place the humanitarian agencies, or at least those that could raise voluntary donations. Historically, some of the agencies function in this manner, while others receive their funding through the "UN system." Nothing is likely to do more to eliminate waste and deadwood while at the same time prompting innovative programming than forcing every UN agency to have to convince donors that what it is doing is worth their money.

The political bodies could be replaced mostly by voluntary or ad hoc ones. In addition to providing an umbrella for the humanitarian agencies, the UN would continue as a gathering place for diplomats from all over, a high-level salon. Nations could still send diplomats to New York, and the delegates' lounge could be enlarged, to provide augmented facilities for the kind of informal communications that could be useful. There might also be facilities available for multilateral meetings of all sizes. If nations had issues on which they wished to express themselves, nothing would stop them from calling a meeting of whomever was interested. This kind of Hyde Park facility would be an improvement over the General Assembly. Since there would be no votes, and meetings would not be automatic, they would have to draw attendance and command attention by dint of the quality of their discourse.

Similarly, nations would be free to form caucuses or clubs. Thus, a group of the democracies could form a committee on human rights that could forthrightly condemn and publicize egregious abuses. True, it would hold no formal authority, but the current Commission on Human Rights has no power to do anything beyond publicizing abuses. Likewise, if the Arab states wished to caucus to calumniate Israel the way the specialized agencies on the Palestinian question currently do, they would be free to do so, but without others having to help foot the bill or lend their imprimatur to the exercise. There might also be a protocol—akin to the procedure set out in the *Uniting for Peace* resolution—by which a nation or group of nations could, in the face of a threat to international peace and security, convene emergency meetings to consider joint action.

It is true that at some moments, Security Council resolutions have been valuable responses to crises, and these would no longer be available. Resolution 242[3] provides an enduring framework for an ultimate settlement between Arabs and Israelis, and resolution 1559[4] contributed significantly to the political pressure that drove Syria from Lebanon. But in such cases, a joint declaration hammered out by a large group of states might have nearly the same value. And, in return, there would no longer be the danger that needed action could be blocked by a veto.

The political and military tasks of keeping the peace that the UN has long failed to fulfill must fall to alliances and coalitions of the willing. This is a lesson that the United States has had to learn from hard experience. Dating at least to President Washington's Farewell Address, America had an aversion to alliances. On Washington's lips this aversion was a form of realism, a reluctance to assume obligations that we might later find burdensome. In the voice of President Wilson, this same standoffishness reappeared as idealism: Alliances were unseemly because they were self-serving. International organization was seen as a purer alternative. This attitude continued into the aftermath of World War II. Winston Churchill wished to form a bipartite alliance in which the peace of the post-1945 world would be policed by the United States and the United Kingdom. But we still felt ourselves too pure for that. Instead, we aimed to transform our wartime alliance—the United Nations—into something nobler, an international organization embracing all.

Shortly thereafter, we also agreed to join an alliance, NATO, which was not our own idea but was sprung from the brow of British foreign minister Ernest Bevin. Following NATO, we formed several other alliances. Some of them failed, but NATO succeeded remarkably. More than any other body, it was responsible for sparing the world from another general war like the two bloody ones that had come before. The UN made no contribution to this deliverance. The lesson is that alliances can be more effective instruments for keeping the peace than international organizations.

Fixing the UN in its security role is hopeless. We have witnessed the tragedy of the failure of the League of Nations, then the failure of the UN during the Cold War, and then the failure of the post–Cold War UN. Three strikes, as they say, and you're out. International organizations have amply proved that they are not reliable instruments for keeping the peace. Instead, in addition to maintaining our own strength, our security strategy should focus on making our primary alliance—NATO—as effective as possible in terms of its military capabilities, the breadth of its responsibilities, and the efficiency of its decision-making structure. Then, too, we ought to see that our other alliances are adequate to sustain our interests in parts of the world that NATO does not touch.

However, one vital role the UN has played that might not be fully replaced by alliance networks is peacekeeping, in the sense of the term I have described above: the process of transition to stable peace in settings where warring parties have agreed to end their hostilities. Ideally, the capacity of regional bodies to perform such functions should be enhanced, as Annan suggests.[5] But there still might be a need for an international peacekeeping capability.

Catherine Bertini, the former undersecretary general for management, has proposed a new "formal governance structure" for the UN's peacekeeping department. She points out that the current budget for peacekeeping operations dwarfs the UN's own operating budget, and that neither the secretariat nor the Security Council is set up to oversee this work.[6] The governing body that Bertini proposes would start with the five permanent members of the Security Council. But this would be moot if the Security Council were abolished. Instead, such a governing body might be made up of whichever nations were prepared to make substantial commitments either of military personnel or of funds.

Who, then, would decide where such peacekeepers would be deployed if there were no Security Council to authorize missions? In most cases, the local parties themselves could request such services from the UN peacekeepers, since we are talking about situations where an end to fighting is agreed. Alternatively, outside mediators, a common fixture of such scenarios, might suggest it. Regional organizations might also request help.

There are other situations in which intervention is desirable to stop humanitarian catastrophes, what Annan calls the "responsibility to protect." But these may, in any case, entail military capabilities greater than UN peacekeepers, with their current resources and rules of engagement, possess. Most of our experience with such situations involves tragedies in which no one did, in fact, intervene, at least not in a timely way, such as the Holocaust, Cambodia, and Rwanda. The closest example of such intervention was the NATO intervention in Kosovo, undertaken without UN approval due to the threat of a Russian veto. As this case points up, it is not clear whether timely humanitarian intervention would be more or less likely in the absence of the Security Council.

Despite all the talk about "unilateralism," it is supremely in America's interests to have friends and partners. Many nations would like to have alliances with us, as an alliance with the United States is the firmest guarantee of security that a nation can have in the contemporary world. While we need not be profligate in making alliances to the point where our commitments outrun our capabilities, we can construct and maintain a network of alliances that will constitute a robust multilateralism more meaningful than the sickly multilateralism of the UN.

Ivo Daalder and James Lindsay have floated the interesting idea of an alliance of democracies. There is already a Community of Democracies, founded at a conference in Warsaw in 2000. But Daalder and Lindsay criticize the flabbiness of its entrance criteria. More than a hundred states belong, including a number that are not democracies by any reasonable definition. The organization they propose would be limited to states meeting a high standard of democratic practice—fewer than sixty, they say. And it would be a real alliance. Unlike the Community of Democracies, which is a loose agglomeration whose sole purpose is to spread democracy, Daalder and Lindsay propose an organization whose purpose would be "to confront common security challenges." And they would reinforce it with an economic dimension, aiming for "eliminating tariffs and other trade barriers among member countries."[7]

An obvious difficulty with this idea is that it would generate friction with countries not invited into the alliance. This, in turn, might give cold feet to those that are invited. The members of the EU, as I noted regarding the proposal for a democracy caucus within the UN, might prove to be too absorbed in the development of that organization. But however difficult it might be to effectuate, this is an innovative approach that deserves careful exploration.

Beyond standing alliances, we can rally "coalitions of the willing" to confront various challenges on an ad hoc basis. This term has come into frequent use in the debate about Iraq, with such coalitions being posited as an alternative to UN-endorsed actions. But this is a false dichotomy. Since the UN's own peace-enforcement machinery has always been a dead letter, on the few occasions when the Security Council has acted to enforce international peace, it has done so by calling forth coalitions of the willing. That is how it handled both Korea and Kuwait.

And, of course, all UN peacekeeping operations are composed of forces volunteered by whichever nations choose to contribute. Whether under UN auspices or not, when the United States acts against a threat to international peace and security, it will inevitably do so by leading a coalition of the willing. The only real question is whether we will do this when we ourselves deem it necessary, or whether we should subject such decisions to a capriciously composed Security Council and the vetoes of Moscow, Paris, and Beijing.

Such voluntarism applies not only to military but also diplomatic activities. Rarely has the Security Council played a part in crisis diplomacy. Instead, numerous times, ad hoc groups of nations have come together to tackle the problems of most interest to them or where they held comparative advantage. Today, the "E3" (France, Germany, and the United Kingdom) negotiate with Iran over its nuclear program, while North Korea's nukes are the subject of six-power talks, and the Middle East peace process is spurred by the "quartet." In the 1990s, efforts to resolve the war in Bosnia were organized by the "contact group," while in the 1980s Central America's wars were negotiated by the Contadora group. And there are numerous other such examples. The involvement in crisis diplomacy by small blocs of interested parties makes more sense than the cumbersome machinery of the UN.

Until we can succeed in overhauling international structures along the lines I have recommended, it is urgent that American administrations persist in the work of affirming a broad construction of article 51 of the UN charter. This was begun by President Bush's *National Security Strategy* paper of September 2002, which outlined the case for "preemptive" self-defense.[8] As noted earlier, some critics pointed out that Bush's approach went beyond traditional notions of preemption to "prevention"; but even a narrow doctrine of preemption is inconsonant with a strict interpretation of article 51. This provision would appear to disallow self-defense except after an armed attack occurs, although, as with most legalisms, there is room to cavil.

Article 51 constitutes part of the core of the charter's law on the use of force. The other key component is article 2.4, which forbids "the threat or use of force against the territorial integrity or political independence" of any state. But this rule is bounded by the "inherent right of individual or collective self-defense" affirmed by article 51, as well as by the provisions in article 42 for the Security Council to undertake the use of force against a state violating international peace and security.

The theory behind all of this—the theory that lies at the very heart of the UN—is an international "social contract" analogous to the Lockean idea that citizens relinquish some of their natural freedom to the state in exchange for the protections it offers. In the international version, states relinquish part of their right to use force in defense of themselves or their interests in exchange for the protections given them by the UN system. This theory was the basis of Kofi Annan's denunciation of the U.S. invasion of Iraq as "illegal" because it lacked the explicit authorization of the Security Council.

However, there is a fatal flaw in this system. The protections that the UN is supposed to offer have proved illusory. Article 42 (which provides for a military response by the Security Council to breaches of the peace) is a dead letter. Indeed, the High-Level Panel and the secretary general implicitly acknowledged this by recommending, among very few amendments to the charter, the abolition of the Military Staff Committee that was supposed to organize the forces at the UN's disposal.[9] It is unlikely that there is a state in the world that trusts the UN to defend it if attacked.

Thus, the social contract on which the UN rests is null and void. The bargain was broken by the UN. It is preposterous to suggest that states must still count themselves as having relinquished part of their freedom of action in exchange for . . . nothing. In practice, what this means is that the apparently narrow wording of article 51 must be given a broad interpretation. Supreme Court Justice Robert H. Jackson once said that the Constitution is not a suicide pact.[10] Neither is the UN charter. Because international law is governed by custom, if the United States insists on this repeatedly, then in effect it will become so, especially since logic is overwhelmingly on our side.

In the reports containing their proposals for UN reform, both the High-Level Panel and the secretary general assert with striking certitude that preemptive war is legitimate. As Mr. Annan puts it, "Imminent threats are fully covered by Article 51. . . . Lawyers have long recognized that this covers an imminent attack as well as one that has already happened."[11] Both Annan and the panel also endorse the legality of war initiated for humanitarian purposes. "As to genocide, ethnic cleansing and other such crimes against humanity, are they not also threats to international peace and against which humanity should be able to look to the Security Council for protection?" asks the secretary general rhetorically.[12]

But neither report accepts the Bush administration's argument about cases such as we faced in Iraq. Annan writes, "Where threats are not imminent but latent, the Charter gives full authority to the Security Council to use military force, including preventively, to preserve international peace and security."[13]

This argument is reasonable but it is not compelling, legally or politically. If articles 2.4 and 51 and 2.7 ("Nothing contained in the present Charter shall authorize the United Nations to intervene in matters which are essentially with the domestic jurisdiction of any state") are not to be read literally but rather to be broadly construed, then the secretary general and the High-Level Panel are not the only ones entitled to interpret them. If the charter does, indeed, envision preemptive self-defense, then it is necessary to address the question raised by President Bush that an imminent threat posed by a weapon of mass destruction in the hands of terrorists may not be visible.

The question is not dismissed by labeling such a threat "latent." Nor does reference to the authority that the charter vests in the Security Council provide a satisfactory answer, in light of the historic failure of the Security Council to play the protective role for which it was created. If the threat of nuclear terrorism is real, as the

High-Level Panel seems to concede, then it will not do to assert that the Security Council will deal with it.[14]

There are some who will say that if the United States interprets the right of self-defense broadly, miscreants will do likewise, using the claim of self-defense to cover actions that are in truth aggressive. But this argument confuses paper barriers with real ones. Miscreants will always make up excuses for their depredations. What stops them is not "the law," but the willingness of others to uphold the law and to stop them. In theory, this job belongs to the United Nations, but in practice, it usually falls to the United States. Giving ourselves a little more freedom will not give bad guys more freedom; it will give them less. What has made the world more peaceful the last half-century, and particularly since 1989, is that the most powerful nation is also a nation that is committed to world order and does not use its power for self-aggrandizement. If the UN is used—as some wish it to be—as a counterweight to the United States, it will turn out to be the enemy of peace and security, rather than its bulwark.

Appendix A

Which United Nations Member Countries Voted Most Often with the United States in the UN General Assembly?

This rank-ordered list of the other 190 member countries of the UN shows how often each voted in accordance with the United States in the General Assembly during 2004. The percentage of each country's votes in agreement with the United States appears in column 2. The voting percentages do not count abstentions or absences and also do not count consensus votes. Column 3 shows each country's freedom rating for 2004 on Freedom House's scale, in which 1 represents most free and 7 least free. Column 4 shows the countries that are called "electoral democracies" by Freedom House.

Country	Frequency of Voting with the United States	Freedom Score	Electoral Democracy
Palau	98.5%	1.0	Yes
Israel	93.2%	2.0	Yes
Micronesia	78.0%	1.0	Yes
Marshall Islands	61.1%	1.0	Yes
United Kingdom	56.7%	1.0	Yes
Australia	56.7%	1.0	Yes
France	54.1%	1.0	Yes
Albania	50.0%	3.0	Yes
Canada	50.0%	1.0	Yes
Kiribati	50.0%	1.0	Yes
Latvia	47.1%	1.5	Yes
Monaco	46.8%	1.5	Yes
Poland	45.7%	1.0	Yes

(continued on next page)

Country	Frequency of Voting with the United States	Freedom Score	Electoral Democracy
Iceland	45.5%	1.0	Yes
Spain	45.5%	1.0	Yes
Denmark	44.9%	1.0	Yes
Czech Republic	44.8%	1.0	Yes
Germany	44.8%	1.0	Yes
Bulgaria	44.1%	1.5	Yes
Romania	44.1%	2.5	Yes
Slovenia	44.1%	1.0	Yes
Belgium	43.9%	1.0	Yes
Finland	43.5%	1.0	Yes
Greece	43.5%	1.5	Yes
Italy	43.5%	1.0	Yes
Lithuania	43.5%	2.0	Yes
Portugal	43.5%	1.0	Yes
Slovak Republic	43.5%	1.0	Yes
Hungary	43.3%	1.0	Yes
Luxembourg	43.3%	1.0	Yes
Japan	42.9%	1.5	Yes
Netherlands	42.9%	1.0	Yes
Austria	42.6%	1.0	Yes
Bosnia and Herzegovina	42.6%	3.5	No
Croatia	42.6%	2.0	Yes
Norway	42.6%	1.0	Yes
Serbia and Montenegro	42.6%	2.5	Yes
Sweden	42.6%	1.0	Yes
Switzerland	42.4%	1.0	Yes
FYR Macedonia	42.4%	3.0	No
Andorra	42.0%	1.0	Yes
Liechtenstein	41.8%	1.0	Yes
Estonia	41.5%	1.0	Yes
Ireland	41.2%	1.0	Yes
San Marino	41.2%	1.0	Yes
New Zealand	40.6%	1.0	Yes
Cyprus	40.3%	1.0	Yes
Malta	40.0%	1.0	Yes
Nauru	39.6%	1.0	Yes
Republic of Korea	39.3%	1.5	Yes

(continued on next page)

Country	Frequency of Voting with the United States	Freedom Score	Electoral Democracy
Georgia	36.7%	3.5	Yes
Republic of Moldova	36.7%	3.5	Yes
Turkey	34.8%	3.0	Yes
Samoa	29.8%	2.0	Yes
Grenada	29.2%	1.5	Yes
Ukraine	28.6%	3.5	Yes
Dem. Rep. of Congo (Kinshasa)	27.3%	6.0	No
Chile	27.0%	1.0	Yes
Armenia	26.9%	4.5	Yes
Nicaragua	26.1%	3.0	Yes
Argentina	25.0%	2.0	Yes
Peru	25.0%	2.5	Yes
Paraguay	24.7%	3.0	Yes
Timor-Leste	24.7%	3.0	No
El Salvador	24.3%	2.5	Yes
Guatemala	23.9%	4.0	Yes
Honduras	23.7%	3.0	Yes
Dominican Republic	23.5%	2.0	Yes
Panama	23.4%	1.5	Yes
Bolivia	23.1%	3.0	Yes
Mexico	23.0%	2.0	Yes
Chad	22.7%	5.5	No
Solomon Islands	22.6%	3.0	Yes
Malawi	22.5%	4.0	Yes
Papua New Guinea	21.6%	3.0	Yes
Cameroon	21.4%	6.0	No
Guinea-Bissau	21.2%	4.0	Yes
Costa Rica	21.1%	1.0	Yes
Uruguay	20.6%	1.0	Yes
Equatorial Guinea	20.4%	6.5	No
India	20.0%	2.5	Yes
Russia	18.6%	5.5	Yes
Fiji	18.5%	3.5	Yes
Haiti	18.2%	6.5	No
Côte d'Ivoire	18.0%	6.0	No
Guinea	17.4%	5.5	No

(continued on next page)

Country	Frequency of Voting with the United States	Freedom Score	Electoral Democracy
Angola	17.3%	5.5	No
St. Kitts and Nevis	16.7%	1.5	Yes
Trinidad and Tobago	16.2%	3.0	Yes
Central African Republic	16.1%	5.5	No
Jordan	16.0%	4.5	No
Ecuador	15.7%	3.0	Yes
Tuvalu	15.2%	1.0	Yes
Namibia	15.1%	2.5	Yes
Benin	14.9%	2.0	Yes
Brazil	14.9%	2.5	Yes
Thailand	14.9%	2.5	Yes
Seychelles	14.9%	3.0	Yes
Nigeria	14.9%	4.0	Yes
Niger	14.8%	3.0	Yes
Mongolia	14.7%	2.0	Yes
Ghana	14.5%	2.0	Yes
Burkina Faso	14.3%	4.5	No
Mali	14.1%	2.0	Yes
Swaziland	14.0%	6.0	No
Ethiopia	13.8%	5.0	No
Singapore	13.6%	4.5	No
Liberia	13.6%	4.5	No
Saint Lucia	13.4%	1.5	Yes
St. Vincent and the Grenadines	13.4%	1.5	Yes
Kyrgyzstan	13.3%	5.5	No
Senegal	13.3%	2.5	Yes
Sudan	13.3%	7.0	No
Guyana	13.0%	2.0	Yes
Philippines	13.0%	2.5	Yes
Sri Lanka	12.9%	3.0	Yes
Djibouti	12.7%	5.0	No
Madagascar	12.7%	3.0	Yes
Nepal	12.7%	5.0	No
Zambia	12.7%	4.0	No
Azerbaijan	12.5%	5.5	No
Botswana	12.5%	2.0	Yes
Jamaica	12.5%	2.5	Yes

(continued on next page)

Country	Frequency of Voting with the United States	Freedom Score	Electoral Democracy
Kenya	12.5%	3.0	Yes
Uzbekistan	12.5%	6.5	No
Sierra Leone	12.1%	3.5	Yes
Vanuatu	12.1%	2.0	Yes
Gabon	12.1%	4.5	No
Gambia	12.0%	4.0	No
Mauritius	11.9%	1.0	Yes
U.R. Tanzania	11.9%	3.5	No
Burma	11.8%	7.0	No
Cambodia	11.8%	5.5	No
Belize	11.6%	1.5	Yes
Morocco	11.4%	4.5	No
South Africa	11.4%	1.5	Yes
Rwanda	11.3%	5.5	No
Togo	11.1%	5.5	No
Venezuela	11.0%	3.5	Yes
Bahamas	10.9%	1.0	Yes
Kazakhstan	10.9%	5.5	No
Tajikistan	10.9%	5.5	No
Antigua and Barbuda	10.7%	2.0	No
Colombia	10.6%	4.0	Yes
Eritrea	10.6%	6.5	No
Maldives	10.1%	5.5	No
Syria	10.1%	7.0	No
Algeria	10.0%	5.5	No
Kuwait	10.0%	4.5	No
Mozambique	10.0%	3.5	Yes
Qatar	10.0%	5.5	No
Tunisia	10.0%	5.5	No
Oman	9.9%	5.5	No
Burundi	9.8%	5.0	No
Libya	9.7%	7.0	No
Pakistan	9.7%	5.5	No
Barbados	9.5%	1.0	Yes
Dominica	9.5%	1.0	Yes
Sao Tome and Principe	9.3%	2.0	Yes
Lesotho	9.0%	2.5	Yes

(continued on next page)

Country	Frequency of Voting with the United States	Freedom Score	Electoral Democracy
Bahrain	8.8%	5.0	No
China	8.8%	6.5	No
Somalia	8.8%	6.5	No
Afghanistan	8.8%	5.5	No
Brunei Darussalam	8.7%	5.5	No
Lebanon	8.7%	5.5	No
Suriname	8.7%	1.5	Yes
Bangladesh	8.6%	4.0	Yes
Malaysia	8.6%	4.0	No
Mauritania	8.6%	5.5	No
Yemen	8.6%	5.0	No
Egypt	8.5%	5.5	No
Iran	8.5%	6.0	No
Indonesia	8.3%	3.5	Yes
Uganda	8.3%	4.5	No
Belarus	8.1%	6.5	No
Cape Verde	8.1%	1.0	Yes
Comoros	8.1%	4.0	No
Tonga	7.9%	4.0	No
United Arab Emirates	7.5%	6.0	No
Cuba	7.4%	7.0	No
Saudi Arabia	7.2%	7.0	No
Zimbabwe	7.2%	6.5	No
Bhutan	7.1%	5.5	No
Congo, Republic of	6.5%	4.5	No
Vietnam	6.0%	6.5	No
Turkmenistan	5.8%	7.0	No
Iraq	5.6%	6.0	No
Laos	5.0%	6.5	No
North Korea	3.3%	7.0	No

SOURCES: Data on UN voting: "Voting Practices in the United Nations, 2004," U.S. Department of State, http://www.state.gov/p/io/rls/rpt/c14622.htm. Data on Freedom House rankings: "Freedom in the World, 2005," Freedom House, http://www.freedomhouse. org/research/freeworld/2005/combined2005.pdf. Data on electoral democracies: "Freedom in the World, 2004," Freedom House, http://www.freedomhouse.org/research/freeworld/ 2004/democracies.pdf.

Appendix B

Odd Man Out or Back Where We Started?

At the time the Cold War ended, other countries in the UN voted in accordance with the United States only 21 percent of the time, on average. Over the next five years, that figure rose to over 50 percent, and then began to fall again. In 2004 it reached as low as 23 percent. These numbers are country averages, excluding abstentions and absences, and consensus resolutions.

Year	Average Concordance with the United States of Votes in the General Assembly
1990	21.30%
1991	27.80%
1992	31.00%
1993	36.80%
1994	48.60%
1995	50.60%
1996	49.40%
1997	46.70%
1998	44.20%
1999	41.80%
2000	43.00%
2001	31.70%
2002	31.20%
2003	25.50%
2004	23.30%

SOURCE: The U.S. Department of State's annual reports, entitled "Voting Practices in the United Nations," for years 1990–2004. The 2004 report can be found at: http://www.state.gov/p/io/rls/rpt/c14622.htm.

Appendix C

The UN's Budget: Who Pays?

The UN's regular budget, which pays for its general administrative expenses as well as many UN agencies, amounted to $3.6 billion for 2004 and 2005 combined, or about $1.8 billion per year. Countries are "assessed" the shares listed below. Peacekeeping is more expensive. For the single fiscal year 2005, the amount budgeted was nearly $3.9 billion. It is paid by a separate assessment. The chart below shows these assessments, too, as well as the combined assessed share for each country. A large portion of UN expenses, including the entire budgets of many UN agencies, is funded not by assessments, but by voluntary contributions. This voluntary spending may exceed the assessed spending, but no one knows, since there is no consolidated record of it, nor is there any record of what each nation's share of it may be.

Country	Regular Budget Share: 2005 = c. $1.8b	Peacekeeping Share: 2005 = c. $3.9b	Combined Share
USA	22.000%	26.8000%	25.2768%
Japan	19.629%	19.6290%	19.6290%
Germany	8.733%	8.7330%	8.7330%
United Kingdom	6.178%	7.5414%	7.1088%
France	6.080%	7.4098%	6.9878%
Italy	4.926%	4.9260%	4.9260%
Canada	2.837%	2.8370%	2.8370%
Spain	2.520%	2.5200%	2.5200%
China	2.070%	2.5200%	2.3772%
Netherlands	1.695%	1.6950%	1.6950%
Republic of Korea	1.808%	1.5187%	1.6105%
Australia	1.606%	1.6060%	1.6060%
Switzerland	1.207%	1.2070%	1.2070%

(continued on next page)

Country	Regular Budget Share: 2005 = c. $1.8b	Peacekeeping Share: 2005 = c. $3.9b	Combined Share
Belgium	1.078%	1.0780%	1.0780%
Sweden	1.001%	1.0010%	1.0010%
Austria	0.867%	0.8670%	0.8670%
Mexico	1.899%	0.3798%	0.8619%
Denmark	0.724%	0.7240%	0.7240%
Brazil	1.534%	0.3068%	0.6962%
Norway	0.685%	0.6850%	0.6850%
Finland	0.535%	0.5350%	0.5350%
Greece	0.534%	0.5340%	0.5340%
Russia	0.466%	0.5600%	0.5302%
Argentina	0.964%	0.2876%	0.5022%
Portugal	0.474%	0.4740%	0.4740%
Israel	0.470%	0.4700%	0.4700%
Saudi Arabia	0.719%	0.2876%	0.4245%
Singapore	0.391%	0.3617%	0.3710%
Ireland	0.350%	0.3500%	0.3500%
Poland	0.464%	0.1392%	0.2423%
New Zealand	0.230%	0.2300%	0.2300%
United Arab Emirates	0.237%	0.2192%	0.2248%
India	0.424%	0.0848%	0.1924%
Turkey	0.376%	0.0752%	0.1707%
Kuwait	0.163%	0.1508%	0.1547%
South Africa	0.294%	0.0588%	0.1334%
Chile	0.225%	0.0450%	0.1021%
Czech Republic	0.184%	0.0552%	0.0961%
Thailand	0.211%	0.0422%	0.0958%
Malaysia	0.205%	0.0410%	0.0930%
Hungary	0.127%	0.0762%	0.0923%
Slovenia	0.083%	0.0830%	0.0830%
Venezuela	0.173%	0.0346%	0.0785%
Luxembourg	0.078%	0.0780%	0.0780%
Iran	0.158%	0.0316%	0.0717%
Colombia	0.156%	0.0312%	0.0708%
Libya	0.133%	0.0333%	0.0649%
Indonesia	0.143%	0.0286%	0.0649%
Qatar	0.064%	0.0592%	0.0607%
Egypt	0.120%	0.0240%	0.0545%

(continued on next page)

Country	Regular Budget Share: 2005 = c. $1.8b	Peacekeeping Share: 2005 = c. $3.9b	Combined Share
Philippines	0.096%	0.0288%	0.0501%
Peru	0.093%	0.0186%	0.0422%
Cyprus	0.039%	0.0390%	0.0390%
Oman	0.071%	0.0213%	0.0371%
Algeria	0.076%	0.0152%	0.0345%
Iceland	0.034%	0.0340%	0.0340%
Brunei Darussalam	0.034%	0.0315%	0.0323%
Romania	0.061%	0.0183%	0.0319%
Slovakia	0.051%	0.0153%	0.0266%
Pakistan	0.056%	0.0112%	0.0254%
Bahrain	0.030%	0.0220%	0.0245%
Uruguay	0.048%	0.0096%	0.0218%
Morocco	0.047%	0.0094%	0.0213%
Lebanon	0.044%	0.0088%	0.0200%
Cuba	0.043%	0.0086%	0.0195%
Nigeria	0.043%	0.0086%	0.0195%
Ukraine	0.040%	0.0080%	0.0182%
Costa Rica	0.039%	0.0078%	0.0177%
Croatia	0.038%	0.0076%	0.0172%
Syria	0.038%	0.0076%	0.0172%
Dominican Republic	0.035%	0.0070%	0.0159%
Tunisia	0.032%	0.0064%	0.0145%
Malta	0.014%	0.0140%	0.0140%
Guatemala	0.030%	0.0060%	0.0136%
Lithuania	0.024%	0.0072%	0.0125%
Tonga	0.027%	0.0054%	0.0123%
Trinidad and Tobago	0.027%	0.0054%	0.0123%
Bahamas	0.013%	0.0117%	0.0121%
Estonia	0.012%	0.0120%	0.0120%
Kazakhstan	0.025%	0.0050%	0.0113%
El Salvador	0.022%	0.0044%	0.0100%
Vietnam	0.021%	0.0042%	0.0095%
Bulgaria	0.017%	0.0051%	0.0089%
Ecuador	0.019%	0.0038%	0.0086%
Panama	0.019%	0.0038%	0.0086%
Serbia and Montenegro	0.019%	0.0038%	0.0086%
Latvia	0.015%	0.0045%	0.0078%

(continued on next page)

Country	Regular Budget Share: 2005 = c. $1.8b	Peacekeeping Share: 2005 = c. $3.9b	Combined Share
Sri Lanka	0.017%	0.0034%	0.0077%
Barbados	0.010%	0.0060%	0.0073%
Iraq	0.016%	0.0032%	0.0073%
Jamaica	0.015%	0.0030%	0.0068%
Uzbekistan	0.014%	0.0028%	0.0064%
Liechtenstein	0.006%	0.0060%	0.0060%
Botswana	0.012%	0.0024%	0.0054%
Paraguay	0.012%	0.0024%	0.0054%
Andorra	0.005%	0.0050%	0.0050%
Jordan	0.011%	0.0022%	0.0050%
Mauritius	0.011%	0.0022%	0.0050%
Côte d'Ivoire	0.010%	0.0020%	0.0045%
North Korea	0.010%	0.0020%	0.0045%
Bolivia	0.009%	0.0018%	0.0041%
Gabon	0.009%	0.0018%	0.0041%
Kenya	0.009%	0.0018%	0.0041%
Bangladesh	0.010%	0.0010%	0.0039%
Burma	0.010%	0.0010%	0.0039%
Cameroon	0.008%	0.0016%	0.0036%
Zimbabwe	0.007%	0.0014%	0.0032%
Sudan	0.008%	0.0008%	0.0031%
Belarus	0.002%	0.0036%	0.0030%
Monaco	0.003%	0.0030%	0.0030%
San Marino	0.003%	0.0030%	0.0030%
FYR Macedonia	0.006%	0.0012%	0.0027%
Namibia	0.006%	0.0012%	0.0027%
U.R. Tanzania	0.006%	0.0006%	0.0023%
Uganda	0.006%	0.0006%	0.0023%
Yemen	0.006%	0.0006%	0.0023%
Albania	0.005%	0.0010%	0.0023%
Azerbaijan	0.005%	0.0010%	0.0023%
Honduras	0.005%	0.0010%	0.0023%
Turkmenistan	0.005%	0.0010%	0.0023%
Antigua and Barbuda	0.003%	0.0018%	0.0022%
Senegal	0.005%	0.0005%	0.0019%
Fiji	0.004%	0.0008%	0.0018%
Ghana	0.004%	0.0008%	0.0018%

(continued on next page)

Country	Regular Budget Share: 2005 = c. $1.8b	Peacekeeping Share: 2005 = c. $3.9b	Combined Share
Ethiopia	0.004%	0.0004%	0.0015%
Nepal	0.004%	0.0004%	0.0015%
Bosnia and Herzegovina	0.003%	0.0006%	0.0014%
Georgia	0.003%	0.0006%	0.0014%
Papua New Guinea	0.003%	0.0006%	0.0014%
Seychelles	0.002%	0.0008%	0.0012%
Dem. Rep. of Congo (Kinshasa)	0.003%	0.0003%	0.0012%
Guinea	0.003%	0.0003%	0.0012%
Haiti	0.003%	0.0003%	0.0012%
Madagascar	0.003%	0.0003%	0.0012%
Armenia	0.002%	0.0004%	0.0009%
Saint Lucia	0.002%	0.0004%	0.0009%
Swaziland	0.002%	0.0004%	0.0009%
Afghanistan	0.002%	0.0002%	0.0008%
Benin	0.002%	0.0002%	0.0008%
Burkina Faso	0.002%	0.0002%	0.0008%
Cambodia	0.002%	0.0002%	0.0008%
Cape Verde	0.002%	0.0002%	0.0008%
Equatorial Guinea	0.002%	0.0002%	0.0008%
Mali	0.002%	0.0002%	0.0008%
Mozambique	0.002%	0.0002%	0.0008%
Zambia	0.002%	0.0002%	0.0008%
Palau	0.001%	0.0005%	0.0007%
Saint Kitts and Nevis	0.001%	0.0003%	0.0005%
Belize	0.001%	0.0002%	0.0005%
Congo, Republic of	0.001%	0.0002%	0.0005%
Dominica	0.001%	0.0002%	0.0005%
Grenada	0.001%	0.0002%	0.0005%
Guyana	0.001%	0.0002%	0.0005%
Kyrgyzstan	0.001%	0.0002%	0.0005%
Marshall Islands	0.001%	0.0002%	0.0005%
Micronesia	0.001%	0.0002%	0.0005%
Mongolia	0.001%	0.0002%	0.0005%
Nauru	0.001%	0.0002%	0.0005%
Nicaragua	0.001%	0.0002%	0.0005%
Republic of Moldova	0.001%	0.0002%	0.0005%

(continued on next page)

Country	Regular Budget Share: 2005 = c. $1.8b	Peacekeeping Share: 2005 = c. $3.9b	Combined Share
St. Vincent and the Grenadines	0.001%	0.0002%	0.0005%
Suriname	0.001%	0.0002%	0.0005%
Tajikistan	0.001%	0.0002%	0.0005%
Timor-Leste	0.001%	0.0002%	0.0005%
Angola	0.001%	0.0001%	0.0004%
Bhutan	0.001%	0.0001%	0.0004%
Burundi	0.001%	0.0001%	0.0004%
Central African Republic	0.001%	0.0001%	0.0004%
Chad	0.001%	0.0001%	0.0004%
Comoros	0.001%	0.0001%	0.0004%
Djibouti	0.001%	0.0001%	0.0004%
Eritrea	0.001%	0.0001%	0.0004%
Gambia	0.001%	0.0001%	0.0004%
Guinea-Bissau	0.001%	0.0001%	0.0004%
Kiribati	0.001%	0.0001%	0.0004%
Laos	0.001%	0.0001%	0.0004%
Lesotho	0.001%	0.0001%	0.0004%
Liberia	0.001%	0.0001%	0.0004%
Malawi	0.001%	0.0001%	0.0004%
Maldives	0.001%	0.0001%	0.0004%
Mauritania	0.001%	0.0001%	0.0004%
Niger	0.001%	0.0001%	0.0004%
Rwanda	0.001%	0.0001%	0.0004%
Samoa	0.001%	0.0001%	0.0004%
Sao Tome and Principe	0.001%	0.0001%	0.0004%
Sierra Leone	0.001%	0.0001%	0.0004%
Solomon Islands	0.001%	0.0001%	0.0004%
Somalia	0.001%	0.0001%	0.0004%
Togo	0.001%	0.0001%	0.0004%
Tuvalu	0.001%	0.0001%	0.0004%
Vanuatu	0.001%	0.0001%	0.0004%

SOURCE: Data on contribution shares: William J. Durch, Victoria K. Holt, Caroline R. Earle, and Moira K. Shanahan, "The Brahimi Report and the Future of UN Peace Operations," the Henry L. Stimson Center, 2003, 123-28.

Appendix D

The Commission on Human Rights: Foxes Guarding the Chicken Coop

Listed here for the years 2001 through 2004 are the world's most oppressive governments based on their scores on the annual Survey of Freedom by Freedom House. These are the countries that scored either 7 or 6.5 on a scale of 1 to 7 in which 1 is the best possible freedom score and 7 is the worst. Each country that was the subject of some kind of resolution by the Commission on Human Rights explicitly or implicitly criticizing its government, and/or was elected as a member of the commission, appears with an "X" beside its name in the appropriate column.

WORLD'S MOST OPPRESSIVE GOVERNMENTS 2004

Country	Freedom score	Subject of CHR resolution	Member of CHR
Burma	7.0		
Cuba	7.0	X	X
Libya	7.0		
North Korea	7.0	X	
Saudi Arabia	7.0		
Sudan	7.0		X
Syria	7.0		
Turkmenistan	7.0	X	
Belarus	6.5	X	
China	6.5		X
Equatorial Guinea	6.5		
Eritrea	6.5		X
Haiti	6.5		
Laos	6.5		
Somalia	6.5		

(continued on next page)

Uzbekistan	6.5	
Vietnam	6.5	
Zimbabwe	6.5	X

WORLD'S MOST OPPRESSIVE GOVERNMENTS 2003

Country	Freedom score	Subject of CHR resolution	Member of CHR
Burma	7.0		
Cuba	7.0	X	X
Libya (Libya held the presidency of the commission)	7.0		X
North Korea	7.0	X	
Saudi Arabia	7.0		X
Sudan	7.0		X
Syria	7.0		X
Turkmenistan	7.0	X	
China	6.5		X
Equatorial Guinea	6.5		
Eritrea	6.5		
Laos	6.5		
Somalia	6.5		
Uzbekistan	6.5		
Vietnam	6.5		X

WORLD'S MOST OPPRESSIVE GOVERNMENTS 2002
(UNITED STATES NOT ON THE COMMISSION)

Country	Freedom score	Subject of CHR resolution	Member of CHR
Burma	7.0		
Cuba	7.0	X	X
Iraq	7.0	X	
Libya	7.0		X
North Korea	7.0		
Saudi Arabia	7.0		X
Sudan	7.0	X	X
Syria	7.0		X

(continued on next page)

Country	Freedom score		Member
Turkmenistan	7.0		
China	6.5		X
Equatorial Guinea	6.5		
Eritrea	6.5		
Laos	6.5		
Somalia	6.5		
Uzbekistan	6.5		
Vietnam	6.5		X

WORLD'S MOST OPPRESSIVE GOVERNMENTS 2001

Country	Freedom score	Subject of CHR resolution	Member of CHR
Afghanistan	7.0		
Burma	7.0		
Cuba	7.0		X
Iraq	7.0		
Libya	7.0		X
North Korea	7.0		
Saudi Arbaia	7.0		X
Sudan	7.0		
Syria	7.0		X
Turkmenistan	7.0		
Bhutan	6.5		
China	6.5		X
Eritrea	6.5		
Laos	6.5		
Rwanda	6.5	X	
Somalia	6.5		
Uzbekistan	6.5		
Vietnam	6.5		X

Source for list of world's most oppressive governments: Freedom House's annual publication, entitled "Freedom in the World," for years 2001–2004. Source for list of countries that were subjects of Commission on Human Rights resolutions: All resolutions passed by the Commission on Human Rights from 2001–2004 can be found on the United Nations website at: http://www.ohchr.org/english/bodies/chr/previous-sessions.htm. Source for list of countries that were elected members of the commission: Membership lists can be found on the United Nations website at: http://www.ohchr.org/english/bodies/chr/membership.htm.

Notes

Introduction

1. For a concise, cogent account see Jan Karski, *The Great Powers and Poland 1919–1945: From Versailles to Yalta* (Lanham, Md.: University Press of America, 1985), 525–34.

2. The White House, *National Security Strategy of the United States* (Washington, D.C.: U.S. Government Printing Office, January 1993), 3.

3. *Washington Post*, "'It's Self-Evident That We . . . Can't Solve All the Problems,'" October 17, 1993.

4. President, Address, "Remarks to the 48th Session of the United Nations General Assembly in New York City," September 27, 1993, *Weekly Compilation of Presidential Documents* 29, no. 39 (October 4, 1993): 1901–8.

5. Boutros Boutros-Ghali, "Empowering the United Nations," *Foreign Affairs* 71, no. 5 (Winter 1992–93): 89.

6. Warren Strobel, "Peacekeepers Do Everything Everywhere," *Washington Times*, July 19, 1992.

7. House Subcommittee on Appropriations for Foreign Operations, Export Financing and Related Programs, *Testimony May 5, 1994, Madeleine K. Albright, Ambassador, House Appropriations/Foreign Operations, Export Financing and Related Programs, FY 95 Foreign Operations Appropriations,* 103rd Cong., 1994, D491–D500.

8. Quoted in William Drozdiak, "Even Allies Resent U.S. Dominance; America Accused of Bullying World," *Washington Post*, November 4, 1997, A01.

9. Tyler Marshall, "Is U.S. Pushing Europe Off World Stage?" *Los Angeles Times*, July 7, 1998, A1.

10. See, for example, Pierre Beylau, "European Defense: Washington Suspicious," *Paris Le Point*, December 14, 1998, 27, trans. by Foreign Broadcast Information Service (FBIS) for *Daily Report*, West Europe,

December 14, 1998; Claude Angeli, "Clinton Uses United Nations and Iraqis as Doormats," *Paris Le Canard Enchaine*, November 18, 1998, 3, trans. by FBIS for *Daily Report*, West Europe, November 18, 1998; Jean-Dominique Merchet: "Allies Split Over NATO Territory," *Paris Liberation*, December 9, 1998, 10, trans. by FBIS for *Daily Report*, West Europe, December 9, 1998.

11. Hubert Vedrine, interview by Jacques Amalric and Pierre Haski, "Vedrine: 'The Era of Symbolism Is Over,'" *Liberation*, November 24, 1998, 8–9, trans. by FBIS for *Daily Report*, West Europe, November 24, 1998.

12. Elaine Sciolino, "Threats and Responses: Perspectives; French Leader Offers Formula to Tackle Iraq," *New York Times*, September 9, 2002, A1.

13. UN Security Council, 4644th Meeting, Resolution 1441, November 8, 2002.

14. M. Dominique de Villepin, "Law, Force and Justice," speech, International Institute for Strategic Studies, London, March 27, 2003, Ministry of Foreign Affairs, Paris, France.

15. BBC News, "Iraq War Illegal, Says Annan," *World Edition*, September 16, 2004.

16. Shashi Tharoor, "Why America Still Needs the United Nations," *Foreign Affairs* 82, no. 5 (September/October 2003): 71.

17. British Broadcasting Corporation, "Vietnam Sees Military Collusion in Kissinger's Visit to China," Hanoi home service, May 10, 1979.

18. Tharoor, "Why America Still Needs the United Nations," 78.

19. Alexander Moens, "Who's Afraid of the Hyperpower?" *Washington Post*, May 14, 2005.

Chapter 1: The Birth of the UN:
A Case of Thoughtless Paternity

1. Townsend Hoopes and Douglas Brinkley, *FDR and the Creation of the U.N.* (New Haven: Yale, 1997), 90.

2. Ibid., 84–85.

3. Stephen C. Schlesinger, *Act of Creation: The Founding of the United Nations* (Boulder: Westview, 2003), 57–58.

4. Hoopes and Brinkley, *FDR and the Creation of the U.N.*, 178–79.

5. Ibid., 59.

6. Ibid., 8.

7. Robert Dallek, *Franklin D. Roosevelt and American Foreign Policy, 1932–1945* (New York: Oxford University Press, 1979), 505.

8. Walter Lippmann, *U.S. War Aims: The Politics and Strategy of World War II* (New York: Da Capo Press, 1976), 64.

9. Ibid., 154.

10. Ibid., 142.

11. George F. Kennan, *American Diplomacy, 1900–1950* (Chicago: University of Chicago Press, 1951), 95.

12. Winston Churchill, *The Grand Alliance*, vol. 3 of *The Second World War* (Boston: Houghton Mifflin, 1950), 444.

13. Anthony Eden, *The Reckoning*, vol. 2 of *The Memoirs of Anthony Eden, Earl of Avon* (Boston: Houghton Mifflin, 1965), 517.

14. Hoopes and Brinkley, *FDR and the Creation of the U.N.*, 72.

15. Cordell Hull to the president, memorandum, December 29, 1943, in Harely Notter, *Postwar Foreign Policy Preparation, 1939–1945* (Washington, D.C.: U.S. Department of State, 1949), 576–77, quoted in Ruth Russell, *A History of the United Nations Charter: The Role of the United States, 1940–1945* (Washington, D.C.: Brookings Institution, 1958), 990–91.

16. Gaddis Smith, *American Diplomacy During the Second World War, 1941–1945* (New York: John Wiley and Sons, 1965), 81.

17. Joseph E. Davies, *Mission to Moscow* (Garden City: Garden City Publishing, 1943), 163.

18. Milovan Djilas, *Conversations with Stalin* (New York: Harcourt, Brace and World, 1962), 114–15.

Chapter 2: After Sixty Years:
Failure on Many Fronts

1. Ridgway to Marshall, October 28, 1946, Ridgway MSS, box 8a, quoted in Jonathan Soffer, "All for One or All for All: The UN Military Staff Committee and the Contradictions within American Internationalism," *Diplomatic History* 21, no. 1 (1997): 62.

2. Abba Eban, "The U.N. Idea Revisited," *Foreign Affairs* 74, no. 5 (September/October 1995): 44.

3. UN General Assembly, Fifth Session, Resolution 377 (V), *Uniting for Peace*, November 3, 1950.

4. See, for example, William Zartman, "The United Nations Response," in *The Six-Day War: A Retrospective*, ed. Richard B. Parker, 75-77 (Gainesville: University Press of Florida, 1996).

5. Michael Oren, *Six Days of War: June 1967 and the Making of the Modern Middle East* (New York: Oxford, 2002), 12.

6. Ibid., 71.

7. Dag Hammarskjöld, private memorandum, August 5, 1957, in Theodore Draper, *Israel and World Politics: The Roots of the Third Arab-Israeli War* (New York: Viking, 1967), 146.

8. Oren, *Six Days*, 73.

9. Anthony Gaglione and Abraham Yeselson, *A Dangerous Place: The United Nations as a Weapon in World Politics* (New York: Grossman Publishers, 1974), 156.

10. UN Security Council, 3009th Meeting, Resolution 713, September 25, 1991.

11. James Dobbins, Seth G. Jones, Keith Crane, Andrew Rathmell, Brett Steele, Richard Teltschik, and Anga Timilsina, *The UN's Role in Nation-Building: From the Congo to Iraq* (Santa Monica: RAND Corporation, 2005), 243.

12. UN Security Council, 3228th Meeting, Resolution 836, June 4, 1993.

13. On Rose, see Joshua Muravchik, "Yellow Rose," *New Republic*, December 5, 1994, 24–25, and Muravchik, *The Imperative of American Leadership: A Challenge to Neo-Isolationism* (Washington, D.C.: AEI Press, 1996), 125–27. On Janvier, see Muravchik, *Imperative*, 110.

14. John Pomfret, "Two U.N. Officials Accuse U.S. of Prolonging War in Bosnia," *Washington Post*, April 30, 1994.

15. UN General Assembly, Fifty-fourth Session, agenda item 42, *The Fall of Srebrenica*, report of the secretary general prepared in pursuance to General Assembly Resolution 53/35, November 15, 1999, par. 59, p. 19.

16. Ibid., par. 246, p. 58.

17. Ibid., par. 240, p. 57.

18. Ibid., par. 304, p. 68.

19. Ibid., par. 264, p. 61.

20. UN Security Council, 3188th Meeting, Resolution 814, March 26, 1993.

21. Douglas Jehl, "Officials Told to Avoid Calling Rwanda Killings 'Genocide,'" *New York Times*, June 10, 1994, 8.

22. President, Address, "Remarks Honoring Genocide Survivors in Kigali, Rwanda," March 28, 1998, *Weekly Compilation of Presidential Documents* 34, no. 13 (March 30, 1998): 495–98.

23. Dore Gold, *Tower of Babble: How the United Nations Has Fueled Global Chaos* (New York: Crown, 2004), 140.

24. Michael Barnett, *Eyewitness to a Genocide: The United Nations and Rwanda* (Ithaca: Cornell University Press, 2002), 79.

25. Romeo Dallaire, interview by Human Rights Watch/FIDH, Toronto, September 16, 1998, quoted in Human Rights Watch, *Leave None to Tell the Story: Genocide in Rwanda*, http://www.hrw.org/reports/1999/rwanda/Geno15-8-01.htm (accessed June 17, 2005).

26. Ibid.

27. Boutros Boutros-Ghali, *An Agenda for Peace*, report of the secretary general pursuant to the statement adopted by the Summit Meeting of the Security Council on January 31, 1992; Boutros Boutros-Ghali, "Supplement to *An Agenda for Peace*: Position Paper of the Secretary-General on the Occasion of the Fiftieth Anniversary of the United Nations," A/50/60, S/1995/1.

28. Boutros-Ghali, "Supplement," par. 6.

29. Ibid., par. 45.

30. Barnett, *Eyewitness*, 117.

31. Mark Bowden, *Black Hawk Down: A Story of Modern War* (New York: Signet, 2001), 249.

32. Keith B. Richburg, "7 Peace Keepers Killed in Somalia," *Washington Post*, September 6, 1993.

33. Madeleine K. Albright, "United Nations," *Foreign Policy*, no. 138 (September/October 2003): 20.

34. UN General Assembly, *The Fall of Srebrenica*, 107.

35. Daniel Patrick Moynihan, *A Dangerous Place* (Boston: Little, Brown, 1975), 89.

36. John Bolton, "The International Atomic Energy Agency: The World's Enforcer or Paper Tiger?" (lecture, American Enterprise Institute, Washington, D.C., September 28, 2004), available at http://www.aei.org/events/filter.all,eventID.911/transcript.asp (accessed July 11, 2005).

37. Mark Gibbs and Ann Maclachlan, "No Bomb-Quantity of HEU in Iraq, IAEA Safeguards Report Indicates," *Nuclear Fuel* 15, no. 17 (August 20, 1990): 8.

38. Khidir Hamza, "Inside Saddam's Secret Nuclear Program," *Bulletin of the Atomic Scientists* 54, no. 5 (September/October 1998): 26–28.

39. Gary Milhollin, "The Iraqi Bomb," *New Yorker*, February 1, 1993.

40. Senate Committee on Foreign Relations, *Nuclear Proliferation: Learning from the Iraq Experience*, 102nd Cong., 1st sess., October 17, 1991, 20.

41. Federation of American Scientists, "Iraqi Nuclear Weapons," in *WMD Around the World*, http://www.fas.org/nuke/guide/iraq/nuke/program.htm (accessed June 17, 2005).

42. Gold, *Tower of Babble*, 116.

43. UN Security Council, statement of IAEA director general Hans Blix in informal consultations regarding Iraq and Resolution 687, July 15, 1991.

44. Michael Z. Wise, "U.N. Panel Downplays Iran's Nuclear Activities," *Houston Chronicle*, February 15, 1992, A24.

45. *New York Times*, "Atom Agency Finds No Threat at Iran's Sites," February 13, 1992, A17.

46. BBC News, "Head of IAEA Rejects American Criticism on IAEA's Treatment of Iran," *BBC Summary of World Broadcasts*, March 2, 1992. Originally reported on IRNA in English, February 27, 1992.

47. See, for example, Claude van England, "Iran Defends Its Pursuit of Nuclear Technology," *Christian Science Monitor*, February 18, 1993, 7.

48. UN International Atomic Energy Agency, Board of Governors, *Implementation of the NPT Safeguards Agreement in the Islamic Republic of Iran*, GOV/2003/69, September 12, 2003.

49. Ibid., GOV/2003/81, November 26, 2003.

50. Ibid., GOV/2004/21, March 13, 2004.

51. Alan Cowell, "Britain Sees Iran's Threats to Resume Nuclear Activity as 'Serious,'" *New York Times*, May 17, 2005, A5.

52. Henry Sokolski, "The Bomb in Iran's Future," *Middle East Quarterly* 1, no. 2 (June 1994), http://www.meforum.org/article/222 (accessed July 7, 2005).

53. Theodore Hirsch, "The IAEA Additional Protocol: What It Is and Why It Matters," *Nonproliferation Review*, Fall-Winter 2004, 143.

54. House Committee on Foreign Affairs, *Management and Mismanagement at the United Nations: Hearings before the Subcommittee on International Security, International Organizations, and Human Rights*, 103rd Cong., 1st sess., 1993, 80.

55. United Nations, "Salaries, Allowances, Benefits, and Job Classification," http://www.un.org/Depts/OHRM/salaries_allowances/salary.htm (accessed June 20, 2005).

56. United States House of Representatives, International Relations Committee, "Hearing on United Nations Reform," testimony of Catherine Bertini, May 19, 2005.

57. Barbara Crossette, "The U.N. at 50: The Challenges; The U.N. at 50: Facing the Task of Reinventing Itself," *New York Times*, October 22, 1995.

58. Ruth Wedgwood, letter to author, May 31, 2005.

59. UN High-Level Panel on Threats, Challenges, and Change, *A More Secure World: Our Shared Responsibility: Report of the Secretary-General's High-Level Panel on Threats, Challenges, and Change*, A/59/565, November 29, 2004, 76.

60. Jacques-Michel Tondre, "Chirac Salutes China's Rise at End of State Visit," Agence France-Presse, May 18, 1997.

61. The *Washington Post*, "France Reaps Its Reward," May 19, 1997, A20.

62. British Broadcasting Corporation, "Sino-French Joint Declaration Signed in Beijing," May 19, 1997, Xinhua news agency, May 16, 1997.

63. Barbara Crossette, "For First Time, U.S. Is Excluded from U.N. Human Rights Panel," *New York Times*, May 4, 2001, A1.

64. Rosemary Righter, *Utopia Lost: The United Nations and World Order* (New York: Twentieth Century Fund, 1995), 272.

65. Ibid.

66. House Subcommittee on International Operations and Human Rights, *The UN and the Sex Slave Trade in Bosnia: Isolated Case or Larger Problem in the U.N. System? Hearing before the Subcommittee on International Operations and Human Rights of the Committee on International Relations*, 107th Cong., 2nd sess., 2002, 10.

67. UN General Assembly, Fifty-ninth Session, agenda items 114, 118, and 127, *Investigation by the Office of Internal Oversight Services into Allegations of Sexual Exploitation and Abuse in the United Nations Organization Mission in the Democratic Republic of the Congo* (A/59/661), January 5, 2005, par. 40, p. 10; par. 39.

68. "War Crimes Lawyers in UN Corruption Probe," *The Lawyer*, October 22, 2001.

69. Madeleine K. Albright to Lee H. Hamilton, 103rd Cong., 2nd sess., *Congressional Record* 140 (August 19, 1994): E1781.

70. Boutros Boutros-Ghali, "We're Fixing the U.N.," *Washington Post*, August 13, 1995, C7.

71. UN Office of Internal Oversight Services, *Report of Investigation into Misconduct and Abuse of Authority of UNHCR*, June 2, 2004, par. 40.

72. Ibid., par. 43.

73. Ibid., par. 60.

74. Ibid., par. 46.

75. Ibid., par. 47.

76. Ibid., par. 49.

77. Ibid., par. 47.

78. Kofi A. Annan to Staff of the Office of the United Nations High Commissioner for Refugees, July 15, 2004.

79. Warren Hoge, "U.N. Refugee Chief Resigns, Denying Charges of Harassment," *New York Times*, February 20, 2005, A3.

80. Agence France-Presse English, "UN Staff Union Mulls No-Confidence Motion against Senior UN Management," November 19, 2004.

81. UN High-Level Panel on Threats, Challenges, and Change, *A More Secure World*.

82. UN Office of Internal Oversight Services, *United Nations Organizational Integrity Survey 2004: Final Report*, prepared by Deloitte Consulting LLP, 28.

83. Senate Permanent Subcommittee on Investigations, *How Saddam Hussein Abused the United Nations Oil-For-Food Program*, Statement by Mark L. Greenblatt, 108th Cong., 2nd sess., 2004, 2.

84. Independent Inquiry Committee into the United Nations Oil-for-Food Programme, *Interim Report—February 3, 2005*, 20–22, http://www.iic-offp.org/documents/InterimReportFeb2005.pdf (accessed June 20, 2005).

85. Ibid., 20.

86. Ibid., 23.

87. Ibid., 25.

88. Ibid., 24.

89. Ibid., 23.

90. Ibid., *Second Interim Report—March 29, 2005*, 26, http://www.iic-offp.org/documents/InterimReportMar2005.pdf (accessed June 20, 2005).

91. Ibid.

92. Ibid., 64.

93. Ibid., 60.

94. Ibid., 66–68.

95. Ibid., 67.

96. Ibid., 69.

97. Ibid.

98. Ibid., 69–70.

99. Ibid., 65.

100. Ibid., 77.

101. Ibid., 42.

102. Andrew Alderson, "Fury at Annan's Son's Link to £6 Million UN Deal," *Sunday Telegraph*, January 24, 1999, C1.

103. Ibid., 78.

104. Colum Lynch, "Former Oil-for-Food Program Investigator Gives Papers to House Panel," *Washington Post*, May 6, 2005, A17.

105. Senate Permanent Subcommittee on Investigations, *How Saddam Hussein Abused the United Nations Oil-For-Food Program*.

106. Claudia Rossett, "The Oil-for-Food Scam: What Did Kofi Annan Know, and When Did He Know It?" *Commentary* 117, no. 5 (May 2004): 17.

107. Ibid., 19.

108. Moynihan, *A Dangerous Place*, 86.

109. Tharoor, "Why America Still Needs the United Nations," 76, 78.

110. Righter, *Utopia Lost*, 45, 47.

111. UN High-Level Panel on Threats, Challenges, and Change, *A More Secure World*, 72.

112. Philip Gourevitch, "The Optimist: Kofi Annan's U.N. Has Never Been More Important and More Imperiled," *New Yorker*, March 3, 2003.

113. Barnett, *Eyewitness*, 12, xii.

114. UN Commission on Human Rights, Forty-ninth Meeting, Resolution 2002/26, April 22, 2002.

115. Ibid.

116. UN Commission on Human Rights, Thirty-ninth Meeting, Resolution 2002/8, April 15, 2002.

117. UN General Assembly, Thirty-seventh Session, Resolution A/RES/37/43, December 3, 1982.

118. *The United Nations and Human Rights, 1945–1995*, United Nations Blue Book Series, vol. 7 (New York: United Nations Department of Public Information, 1995), 13.

119. UN High-Level Panel on Threats, Challenges, and Change, *A More Secure World*, par. 283, p. 70.

120. UN General Assembly, *In Larger Freedom, Towards Development, Security and Human Rights for All*, Report of the Secretary General, A/59/2005, March 21, 2005, par. 182, p. 45.

121. Tom Lantos, "The Durban Debacle: An Insider's View of the UN World Conference on Racism at Durban," *Fletcher Forum of World Affairs* 26, no. 1 (Winter/Spring 2002): 5.

122. Permanent Mission of Israel to the United Nations, "Israel and the UN–An Uneasy Relationship," http://www.israel-un.org/israel_un/uneasyrelation.htm (accessed July 10, 2005).

123. UN Division for Palestinian Rights, *The Origins and Evolution of The Palestine Problem 1917–1988*, part 1: 1917-1947 (1978), http://domino.un.org/unispal.nsf/9a798adbf322aff38525617b006d88d7/57c45a3dd0d46b09802564740045cc0a!OpenDocument (accessed July 10, 2005).

124. Ibid.

125. Harris Okun Schoenberg, *A Mandate for Terror: The United Nations and the PLO* (New York: Shapolsky, 1989), 481.

126. Ibid.

127. Matthew Levitt, "Terror on the UN Payroll?" *Peacewatch*, no. 475, Washington Institute for Near East Policy, October 13, 2004, 2.

128. United Press International, "Canada Seeks Clarity on U.N.-Hamas Link," October 4, 2004.

129. Quoted in Milton Viorst, *UNRWA and Peace in the Middle East* (Washington, D.C.: Middle East Institute, 1984), 39–40.

130. Lantos, "Durban Debacle," 16.

131. UN General Assembly, Thirtieth Session, Resolution 3379 (XXX), November 10, 1975.

132. Moynihan, *Dangerous Place*, 182.

133. UN General Assembly, Twenty-fifth Session, Resolution 2708 (XXV), December 14, 1970.

134. Colum Lynch, "Islamic Group Blocks Terror Treaty; Nations Demand U.N. Pact Exemption for Anti-Israeli Militants," *Washington Post*, November 10, 2001.

135. Ibid., "U.N. Approves Anti-Terrorism Initiative; In 15–0 Vote, Security Council Urges Nations to Prosecute Offenders and Supporters," *Washington Post*, October 9, 2004, A26.

136. UN High-Level Panel on Threats, Challenges, and Change, *A More Secure World*, 41.

137. Ibid., 45.

138. UN General Assembly, *In Larger Freedom,* par. 91.

139. Quoted by Gamani Corea, "11th Lecture, 2001: Tribute to Raul Prebisch" (Prebisch Lecture Series, United Nations Conference on Trade and Development, Geneva, October 11, 2001).

140. Group of Seventy-Seven at the United Nations, "Aims," website homepage, http://www.g77.org/main/main.htm (accessed June 20, 2005).

141. UN General Assembly, Twenty-ninth Session, Resolution 3281 (XXIX), December 12, 1974.

142. Ibid.

143. Ibid.

144. Ibid.

145. Richard N. Gardner, "The United Nations Conference on Trade and Development," *International Organization* 22, no. 1 (Winter 1968): 101.

146. World Bank, *Tanzania Country Assistance Evaluation*, Report No. 20902-TA (Washington, D.C.: World Bank, September 13, 2000).

147. See Joshua Muravchik, *Heaven on Earth: The Rise and Fall of Socialism* (San Francisco: Encounter Books, 2002), chap. 8 and app. 2.

Chapter 3: Some Areas of Success

1. Dobbins et al., *The UN's Role in Nation-Building*, xvi–xvii.

2. Ibid., xxi.

3. Ibid., xxxv.

4. UN Department of Peacekeeping Operations, "Monthly Summary of Contributors of Military and Civilian Police Personnel," http://www.un.org/ Depts/dpko/dpko/contributors/2005/may2005_1.pdf.

5. Donald G. McNeil Jr., "Polio Detected in Indonesia, Indicating It Crossed an Ocean," *New York Times*, May 2, 2005.

6. Righter, *Utopia Lost*, 296.

7. Jan Egeland, "Sobering Lessons for the United Nations," *Financial Times*, March 30, 2005, 17.

8. Nick Papps, "Downer Accuses UN of Acting Too Slowly," *Courier Mail* (Queensland, Australia), January 21, 2005, 8.

9. Roger Bate, "WHO's to Blame?" *National Review*, February 14, 2005, 30.

10. Pierre Huguenin, "Le Nobel de Kadhafi," *L'Hebdo*, April 27, 1989.

11. Agence France-Presse English, "Swiss Human Rights Campaigner Turns Down 'Kadhafi' Award," October 1, 2002.

12. Tharoor, "Why America Still Needs the United Nations," 76.

13. UN General Assembly, Panel of Eminent Persons on United Nations–Civil Society Relations, *We the Peoples: Civil Society, the United Nations and Global Governance: Report of the Panel of Eminent Persons on United Nations–Civil Society Relations*, A/58/817, June 11, 2004, par. 37, p. 30.

14. Walter Cronkite, *A Reporter's Notebook* (New York: Knopf, 1996), 128.

Chapter 4: Sources of Failure

1. Righter, *Utopia Lost*, 240.

2. Ibid., 127.

3. Barnett, *Eyewitness*, 88, 149; Associated Press Worldstream, "French Troops Criticized for Lack of Action in Rwanda," April 3, 1998; Associated Press Worldstream, "Former Prime Minister Denies French Role in Rwandan Genocide," April 6, 1998.

4. Barnett, *Eyewitness*, 121.

5. Freedom House, "Russia Downgraded to 'Not Free,'" press release, December 20, 2004, http://www.freedomhouse.org/media/pressrel/122004.htm (accessed July 10, 2005).

6. Aili Piano and Arch Puddington (eds.), *Freedom in the World 2004* (Lanham, Md.: Rowman & Littlefield, 2004), 7, 3.

7. Marc Lacey, "U.S. Attacks Rights Group for Ousting It as a Member," *New York Times*, May 5, 2001, A4.

8. UN High-Level Panel on Threats, Challenges, and Change, *A More Secure World*, 70.

9. UN Security Council, 2395th Meeting, Resolution 520, September 17, 1982.

10. International Court of Justice, "Reparation for Injuries Suffered in the Service of the United Nations," I.C.J. Report 174 (The Hague, Netherlands: International Court of Justice, 1949).

11. Righter, *Utopia Lost*, 80.

12. Barnett, *Eyewitness*, 20.

13. Ibid., 14.

14. Righter, *Utopia Lost*, 115.

15. Hoopes and Brinkley, *FDR and the Creation of the U.N.*, 72.

Chapter 5: Proposals for Reform:
Hope Springs Eternal

1. UN High-Level Panel on Threats, Challenges, and Change, *A More Secure World*.

2. UN General Assembly, *In Larger Freedom*.

3. UN General Assembly, Panel of Eminent Persons on United Nations–Civil Society Relations, *We the Peoples*.

4. UN General Assembly, Fifty-seventh Session, item 53 of the provisional agenda: "Strengthening of the United Nations System," A/57/387, September 9, 2002.

5. Kofi A. Annan, *Millenium Report of the Secretary-General of the United Nations: We the Peoples: The Role of the United Nations in the 21st Century*, A/54/2000, March 27, 2000.

6. UN General Assembly, Fifty-first Session, agenda item 168: "United Nations Reform, Measures and Proposals," A/51/950, July 14, 1997.

7. UN General Assembly, Forty-eighth Session, Resolution A/RES/48/162, December 20, 1993.

8. Edward C. Luck, "UN Reform: A Cause in Search of a Constituency," prepared for the Bureau of International Organization Affairs and the Bureau of Intelligence and Research, U.S. Department of State and the National Intelligence Council, Conference on UN Reform, "Forging a Common Understanding," May 6, 2004, 1, http://www.sipa.columbia.edu/cio/cio/projects/LuckUNRefMay6.pdf (accessed June 20, 2005).

9. Rosemary Righter, "How to Bring the UN Back to Life," The *Times* (London), December 3, 2004.

10. Jeffrey Laurenti, "The Geopolitical Rorschach Test: 'Reform' at the United Nations" (Conference, U.S Department of State, Washington, D.C., May 6, 2004), 2–7.

11. House Committee on Foreign Affairs, *Management and Mismanagement at the United Nations*, 77, 85, 100. [The phrase "burdened with an

inordinate . . ." is on p. 77; "almost surreal" is on p. 85; "totally lacking . . ." is on p. 100.]

12. U.S. General Accounting Office, *United Nations: Reforms Progressing, but Comprehensive Assessments Needed to Measure Impact*, report to congressional requesters, GAO-04-339 (Washington, D.C.: U.S. General Accounting Office, 2004), 4–5.

13. UN General Assembly, *In Larger Freedom*, par. 190, 191, 46.

14. Mike Allen and Colum Lynch, "House Backs Withholding Dues to Spur U.N. Changes," *Washington Post*, June 18, 2005, A01.

15. UN General Assembly, *In Larger Freedom*, par. 192, p. 47.

16. Barnett, *Eyewitness*, 31.

17. Panel on United Nations Peace Operations, "Report of the Panel on United Nations Peace Operations," A/55/305-S/2000/809, August 17, 2000.

18. David Hannay, "Reforming the United Nations: The Use of Force to Safeguard International Peace and Human Rights: Recommendations of the Secretary-General's High-Level Panel on Threats, Challenges, and Change: A Member's Perspective" (lecture, Northwestern University School of Law, Chicago, January 24, 2005), 6.

19. Marc Lacey, "U.N. Forces Using Tougher Tactics to Secure Peace," *New York Times*, May 23, 2005, A1.

20. UN High-Level Panel on Threats, Challenges, and Change, *A More Secure World*, 85.

21. Ibid., 82.

22. Ibid., 68.

23. UN General Assembly, Panel of Eminent Persons on United Nations–Civil Society Relations, *We the Peoples*, 16.

24. Ibid., 8.

25. UN High-Level Panel on Threats, Challenges, and Change, *A More Secure World*, 61.

26. Ibid.

27. UN General Assembly, *In Larger Freedom*, par. 160, p. 41.

28. UN High-Level Panel on Threats, Challenges, and Change, *A More Secure World*, p. 10.

29. Ibid., par. 70, p. 22.

30. Ibid., par. 10, p. 4.

31. UN High-Level Panel on Threats, Challenges, and Change, *A More Secure World*, 62.

32. UN General Assembly, *In Larger Freedom*, par. 169, p. 42.

33. Council on Foreign Relations and Freedom House, *Enhancing U.S. Leadership at the United Nations: Report of an Independent Task Force*

Cosponsored by the Council on Foreign Relations and Freedom House, November 2002.

34. See Joshua Muravchik, "Voting Patterns in the United Nations: A Background Report," prepared for the Council on Foreign Relations/ Freedom House Task Force on Enhancing U.S. Leadership at the UN, June 2002, 4–6.

35. UN High-Level Panel on Threats, Challenges, and Change, *A More Secure World*, 2.

36. Ibid., 14.

37. Ibid., 29.

38. Ibid., 73.

39. The White House, *The National Security Strategy of the United States of America*, September 2002, http://www.whitehouse.gov/nsc/nssintro.html (accessed July 10, 2005).

340. UN High-Level Panel on Threats, Challenges, and Change, *A More Secure World*, 51.

41. UN General Assembly, *In Larger Freedom*, par. 124–26, p. 33.

42. UN High-Level Panel on Threats, Challenges, and Change, *A More Secure World*, 18.

43. Ibid., 50.

44. Ibid., 67.

45. UN General Assembly, *In Larger Freedom*, par. 8, p. 4.

46. Ibid., par. 138, p. 36.

47. Ibid., par. 136, p. 356.

48. Ibid., par. 94, p. 27.

49. Ibid.

50. Ibid., par. 182, p. 45.

51. Ibid., par. 23, p. 7.

52. Ibid., par. 17, p. 6.

53. Ibid., par. 28, p. 8.

Chapter 6: A Better Approach

1. Arnold Wolfers, *Discord and Collaboration* (Baltimore: Johns Hopkins University Press, 1962), p. 73.

2. Tim Wirth, interview by Ben Wattenberg, *Think Tank*, PBS, September 16, 2004.

3. UN Security Council, 1382nd Meeting, Resolution 242, November 22, 1967.

4. Ibid., 5028th Meeting, Resolution 1559, September 2, 2004.

5. Ibid., par. 112, p. 31.

6. House Committee on International Relations, *Reforming the United Nations: Budget and Management Perspectives*, 109th Congress, 1st sess., 2005, testimony of Catherine Bertini, http://wwwc.house.gov/international_ relations/109/ber051905.pdf (accessed July 10, 2005).

7. Ivo Daalder and James Lindsay, "Our Way or the Highway: The UN and NATO Have Grown Hopelessly Outdated and are Ill-Equipped to Face Today's Humanitarian and Security Challenges," *Financial Times*, November 6, 2004.

8. The White House, *National Security Strategy*, https://www.whitehouse.gov/nsc/nss.html (accessed July 10, 2005).

9. UN High-Level Panel on Threats, Challenges, and Change, *A More Secure World*, par. 300, p. 73; UN General Assembly, *In Larger Freedom*, par. 219, p. 52.

10. *Terminiello v. Chicago*, 337 U.S. 1, 37 (1949).

11. UN General Assembly, *In Larger Freedom*, par. 124, p. 33. Similarly, UN High-Level Panel on Threats, Challenges, and Change, *A More Secure World*, par. 188, p. 50.

12. UN General Assembly, *In Larger Freedom*, par. 125, p. 33.

13. Ibid.

14. UN High-Level Panel on Threats, Challenges, and Change, *A More Secure World*, par. 189–90, 90, pp. 50–51.

Index

Abdelnour, Fakery, 51
Accountability, UN's lack of,
   86–89
Additional Protocol, IAEA's,
   41–42
Affirmative action and UN inef-
   ficiency, 96
Africa
   Congo crisis (1960-1964), 90
   peacekeeping accomplish-
     ments in, 74–75
   Somalia debacle (1990s), 29,
     32–33, 74
   Sudan and Darfur crisis, 60,
     75, 83
   See also Rwanda genocide
     (1990s)
African Group, political protec-
   tion of rogue members, 60
African Middle East Petroleum
   (AMEP), 50–51
An Agenda for Peace (Boutros-
   Ghali), 31
Aidid, Mohamed Farah, 29
Akashi, Yashushi, 26, 27
Albright, Madeleine, 2, 33, 47
Alliances
   as alternative to UN, 11–12
   effectiveness of, 114–115

importance for U.S., 117
   regional, 8, 11, 14, 91, 104
   U.S. aversion to, 11, 12, 115
   and U.S. peacekeeping suc-
     cesses, 110
AMEP (African Middle East
   Petroleum), 50–51
Amer, Abdul Hakim, 21
Annan, Kofi
   and accountability issue, 88
   concerns about U.S. unilateral
     action, 4, 107
   defense of sexual harassment
     perpetrator, 48
   integrity questions on, 58
   on military action justifica-
     tions, 120
   and oil-for-food program
     scandal, 48–49, 53–56
   and peacekeeping role of UN,
     33
   reform agenda, 92, 94, 99
   and terrorism, 67–68, 108
Annan, Kojo, 51–53, 54
Anti-Americanism
   European, 83–86
   in humanitarian programs, 78
   and Security Council reforms,
     102

Anti-Semitism, UN downplaying of, 65
Anti-Westernism
  in humanitarian programs, 78
  in Non-Aligned Movement, 82
  and resentment among developing countries, 69
  and Security Council reforms, 102
Arab Human Development Report, 79
Arab Lawyers Union, 65
Arab League, political clout in UN, 66
Arafat, Yasir, 67
Article 2.4 on use of force, 119, 120
Article 42 on Security Council's use of force, 119, 120
Article 51 on self-defense, 9, 19–20, 105, 118–120
Asian economies and free market road to development, 71–72
Assertive multilateralism, 2, 33
Attalah, Nahed Rashid Ahmed, 64
Aviation regulation, UN's, 76

Balfour Declaration, 62–63
Barnett, Michael, 32, 58, 90, 97
Bate, Roger, 78
Becirovic, Ramiz, 27
Bevin, Ernest, 13, 115
Blix, Hans, 36, 37
Bokasa, Jean-Bedel, 4
Bolton, John, 34
Bosnia-Herzegovina, 24, 25–29
Bosnian/Serb conflict, 23–24, 25–29, 46, 85, 91

Boutros-Ghali, Boutros
  on OIOS, 47
  and peacekeeping failures, 31–32
  post-Cold War opportunities for UN, 2
  on reform of UN, 92–93, 94
  and Rwandan genocide, 85, 90
  and Somalia debacle, 29
  U.S. opposition to, 58
Brahimi, Lakhdar, 98
Bribery in oil-for-food program, 50
Brinkley, Douglas, 8, 9, 10
Britain, Great
  attempts to make UN more pragmatic, 9
  attitudes toward international organizations, 8, 10, 13, 14, 91, 115
  and politics of Security Council membership, 19
  U.S. concerns about imperialism from, 15–16
Budget, UN, 43–44, 89, 96, 111–112, 130–135
Bureaucratic inertia, 28, 43, 56–57, 77, 94–97
Bush, George H. W., 1–2, 29
Bush, George W., 4, 105, 118
Buyout option for UN "deadwood," 95–96

Cambodia, peacekeeping challenges in, 73–74
Capitalism, UN suspicion of, 82, 108
Cattan, Henry, 63
Charter, UN, erosion of principles, 84

Charter of Economic Rights and
Duties of States, 70
Chechen separatists and terrorism
definition, 67
Chiang Kai-shek, 19
China
and human rights, 45, 60
and Korean War, 19
and politics of Security Coun-
cil membership, 18
response to SARS, 76
unilateral use of force by, 5
Chirac, Jacques, 3, 45
Churchill, Winston, 8, 10, 13, 14,
91, 115
Civil society idea, 99–100
Civil warfare, reductions in, 105,
110–111
Clinton, Bill, 2, 29, 30, 91
Coalitions of willing partners, ad
hoc, 117–118
Cold War, 1, 23, 75, 110, 111
Collective security, 106, 117
See also Regional alliances
Colonialism, Western, and Third
World resentment, 69, 82
Commission on Global Governance, 93
Commission on Human Rights
and capabilities reforms in
UN, 99
establishment of, 9
France's scheme to remove
U.S. from, 86
hypocrisies of, 45, 59–61, 83,
136–138
inability to target specific
governments, 58
and political reforms, 101
and vote-trading practices, 88

Commitment to peace and Security
Council reassurance role,
25, 33, 73–75
Common values, assumption of,
14–15, 84
Communication among nations,
UN as center for, 113–114
Communist nations, See China;
Soviet Union
Community of Democracies, 117
Concert of Europe, 11
Congo crisis (1960-1964), 90
Congress, U.S., reluctance to sup-
port Persian Gulf War, 2
Corruption in UN, 42–58
Cotecna Company, 51–53
Council of Foreign Relations, 103
Cronkite, Walter, 80

Daalder, Ivo, 117
Dallaire, Gen. Romeo, 30–31
Dallek, Robert, 11
Darfur, Sudan crisis, 60, 75, 83
Davies, Joseph, 16
Democracy
alliance of democracies proposal, 117
and changes in UN's political
makeup, 86–87
democracy caucus proposal,
103–104
and global governance,
99–100
popularity among Arab intellectuals, 79
UN as fosterer of, 79–80
U.S. idealism about, 12
Deng Xiaoping, 5
Dependency theory, economic,
69

Developing vs. developed nations, 69–72, 81–83, 84, 101, 108–109
Dictatorial/totalitarian regimes, 84–85, 86
Diplomacy, UN as center for, 114
Diplomatic immunity for UN staff, 43
Disarmament, Iraq's games with, 3–4
Disease treatment and prevention, UN programs for, 76
Distribution vs. production of wealth, 82–83
Division of Palestinian Rights, 62
Downer, Alexander, 77–78
Duelfer, Charles, 54
Duncan, Miranda, 54

Eastern Europe, sacrifice of in birth of UN, 8
East Timor, peacekeeping challenges in, 74
Eban, Abba, 18
Economic issues
  and alliance of democracies, 117
  developing vs. developed nations, 69–72, 81–83, 84, 101, 108–109
Economic Social Council (ECOSOC), 9, 88
Eden, Anthony, 8, 9, 13
Effectiveness, reforms for UN, 97–100
Efficiency, proposals for increased, 94–97
Egeland, Jan, 77
Egypt, 21–22, 83
El Salvador, nation-building in, 74

Embargoes/sanctions, 24, 25–26, 39–40, 48–56
Equity, global economic, as UN goal, 70
Europe
  anti-Americanism of, 83–86
  fears of U.S. international hegemony, 3
  French attitudes, 3–4, 18, 20, 45, 85–86
  post-WWII proposal for European commission, 8
  See also Britain, Great
European Union, 60, 103

Featherbedding in UN staff, 43–44
Federation of American Scientists, 36
Force, use of, 4, 9, 105, 118–121
  See also Peacekeeping
France
  fears of U.S. international hegemony, 3–4
  and Korean War, 20
  opposition to U.S. interests, 85–86
  and politics of Security Council membership, 18
  unilateral use of force by, 4
  and vote-trading, 45
Freedom House, 59, 86, 87, 103
Freedom of speech, UN's attempt to suppress, 84–85
Free market principles in UN, 113
Funding of UN, 43–44, 89, 96, 111–112, 130–135

Gaglione, Anthony, 23
Garaudy, Roger, 78
Gardner, Richard, 71

General Accounting Office (GAO),
U.S., 94–95
General Assembly
abolishment of, 113
anti-Israel bias of, 65–66
and Korean War, 20
NAM, 39, 66, 81–83, 90, 104
as pillar of UN organization,
14
and political reforms, 100
Geneva group of UN members,
43–44
Genocide, *see* Rwanda genocide
(1990s)
Germany, fears of U.S. interna-
tional hegemony, 3
Globalism vs. isolationism for
U.S., 7, 10–11, 13
Gold, Dore, 66–67
Gorbachev, Mikhail, 23
Gourevitch, Philip, 58
Group of Seventy-Seven (G-77),
69–70, 71

Hamas members in UNRWA, 64
Hammarskjöld, Dag, 21, 22, 90
Hamza, Khidir, 35
Hannay, Lord David, 98
Hansen, Peter, 64
Health, public, UN programs,
76–77, 78
Helms-Biden bill to reduce U.S.
UN dues, 96
High Commissioner for Refugees,
46, 77, 88
High-Level Panel on Threats,
Challenges, and Change,
57, 68, 88, 92–109
Hiring system, UN, 94–95
Hirsch, Theodore, 41

Hocké, Jean-Pierre, 77
Hoopes, Townsend, 8, 9, 10
Hull, Cordell, 8, 15
Humanitarian services/agencies
anti-Americanism in, 78
and military action justification,
120
poverty relief, 57, 69–72,
108–109
and success of UN regulatory
agencies, 76–77
UN role in, 112–113, 116–117
Human rights
leftist twisting of, 78
NAM and hypocrisy on, 83
reform of UN role in, 114
and terrorism definitions,
107–108
UN accomplishments, 79
vs. UN politics, 45, 58, 59–61
See also Commission on
Human Rights
Human Rights Watch and Rwanda
genocide, 31
Hunger, combating, 77
Huntington, Samuel, 11
Hutu slaughter of Tutsi opposition in Rwanda, 30–31

IAEA (International Atomic Ener-
gy Agency), 34–42
Idealism, American, 1, 9, 12, 14
IMF (International Monetary
Fund), 101
Imperialism
fears of U.S., 2–3, 15–16
as outgrowth of capitalism, 82
U.S.'s lack of imperialistic
motives, 111, 112
Import-substitution, 69

Independent Inquiry Committee into the United Nations Oil-for-Food Programme, 50–56

Independent Working Group on the Future of the United Nations, 92–93

India, 4, 104

Individual rights vs. states rights, 70–71

Influence vs. imperialism, 111

In Larger Freedom: Towards Development, Security, and Human Rights for All (Annan), 92

International Atomic Energy Agency (IAEA), 34–42

International Civil Aviation Organization, 76

International Criminal Court, 107

Internationalism vs. isolationism for U.S., 7, 10–11, 13

International Monetary Fund (IMF), 101

International organizations
vs. alliances, 115
U.S. idealism about, 1, 9, 12, 14
U.S. post-WWII focus on, 8

International Telecommunications Union, 75–76

Interstate warfare, reductions in, 105

Intrinsic value argument for UN, 79–80

Iran and nuclear nonproliferation deceptions, 37–40

Iranian People's Mojahedin, 37

Iraq
disarmament games, 3–4

France's opposition to U.S. policy concerning, 85

Kuwait invasion, 1–2, 23, 33–34

and nuclear nonproliferation deceptions, 34–37

and oil-for-food program scandal, 48–56

and Security Council's relationship to U.S., 106

Islamic Conference, 66, 67–68

Isolationism vs. internationalism, U.S., 7, 10–11, 13

Israeli-Palestinian conflict
NAM scapegoating of Israel, 83
UN as mediator in, 91
UN role in Six-Day War, 21–22
and UN's anti-Israel bias, 61, 62–67, 78

Italy, biases in Somalia debacle, 32–33

Jackson, Robert H., 119

Janvier, Bernard, 26

Japan, incompetence of WHO chief, 45–46

Jennekens, Jon, 35, 37

Jiang Zemin, 45

Kay, David, 35, 36

Kennan, George, 12

Khmer Rouge, 73–74

Korean War, 19–20

Kosovo conflict and NATO's independent action, 4
See also Bosnian/Serb conflict

Kuwait, Iraqi invasion of, 1–2, 23, 33–34

Lamers, Karl, 3
Lang, Jack, 85
Lantos, Tom, 65
Laurenti, Jeffrey, 93–94
League of Nations, 1, 8, 10, 12
Lebanon, Syria's virtual occupation of, 89
Legalistic/moralistic approach to international issues, criticism of, 12
L'Empire, 78
Lindsay, James, 117
Lippman, Walter, 11–12
Lubbers, Ruud, 47–48, 49, 77
Luck, Edward, 93

Mao Zedong, 19
Marshall Plan, 110
Massey, Elie, 52, 53
Massey, Robert, 52, 53
McKenzie, Lewis, 97
Meritocracy, UN's lack of, 44, 96
Middle East crises, *see* Israeli-Palestinian conflict
Milhollin, Gary, 35
Milieu vs. possession goals of nations, 111
Military action, UN's attitudes toward, 1–2, 9, 18–19, 105, 118–121
See also Peacekeeping
Military Staff Committee (MSC), 17–18, 119
Millennium Summit, 92
Moens, Alexander, 5
Molotov, Vyachislav, 8
Monroe Doctrine, 11
Moral leadership and corruption in UN, 42–58

Moynihan, Daniel Patrick, 34, 56, 65
MSC (Military Staff Committee), 17–18, 119
Muammar Qaddafi Human Rights Prize, 78
Multilateralism
    assertive, 2, 33
    as balance to U.S. power, 3
    as intrinsic value, 79, 113
    and robust alliances, 117

NAM (Non-Aligned Movement), 39, 66, 81–83, 90, 104
Nasser, Gamal Abdel, 21
Nationalist Chinese government, 19
Nationalization of economic power, 70
National Security Strategy (Bush, H. W.), 118
Nation-building, UN vs. U.S. in, 74
NATO (North Atlantic Treaty Organization), 4, 13, 28, 115
New International Economic Order (NIEO), 70
New World Information and Communication Order, 84–85
NGOs (nongovernmental organizations), 61, 99–100
NIEO (New International Economic Order), 70
Nigerian forces in Somalia, 32–33
Non-Aligned Movement (NAM), 39, 66, 81–83, 90, 104
Nongovernmental organizations (NGOs), 61, 99–100
Nonproliferation, nuclear, 34–42

Non-Proliferation Treaty (NPT),
34, 37–40, 41
North Atlantic Treaty Organization
(NATO), 4, 13, 28, 115
North Korea and nuclear nonpro-
liferation deceptions, 41
Norway and NATO action in Ser-
bia, 4
NPT (Non-Proliferation Treaty),
34, 37–40, 41
Nuclear nonproliferation, 34–42
Nyerere, Julius, 71

Office of Internal Oversight Ser-
vices (OIOS), 46–49
Ogata, Sadako, 77
Oil-for-food program, corruption
in, 48–56
OIOS (Office of Internal Over-
sight Services), 46–49
Optional Protocol, IAEA's, 42
Oren, Michael, 22
Organization of the Islamic Con-
ference, 66, 67–68
The Origins and Evolution of the
Palestine Problem (Division
of Palestinian Rights),
62–63
Oversight authority and oil-for-
food program problems,
54–55

Palestinian-Israeli conflict, see
Israeli-Palestinian conflict
Panel of Eminent Persons on
United Nations–Civil
Society Relations, 92, 99
Parton, Robert, 54
Pax Americana vs. pax UN, 5
Peacebuilding Commission, 98

Peacekeeping
alliances and coalitions as
superior agents of, 114–115
alternatives to UN structure,
116–119
and effectiveness of UN,
104–105
reforms in UN, 97–99
UN disappointments in, 2,
17–34
UN successes, 73–75
U.S. vs. UN contribution to,
110–112
See also Security Council
People's Mojahedin, 37
Pérez de Cuellar, Javier, 58
Persian Gulf War, 1–2, 23, 33–34
Petrovsky, Vladimir, 2
Politics
and democracy's growth, 86–87
vs. humanitarian work of UN,
112–113
vs. human rights, 45, 58,
59–61
and pro-Palestinian bias of
UN, 62–67
and reform of UN, 100–106,
113–114
of Security Council membership, 18–19
and UN staff positions, 43–45
Possession vs. milieu goals of
nations, 111
Postal regulation, UN's, 76
Poverty, 57, 69–72, 108–109
Powell, Colin, 64
Prebisch, Raul, 69
Preemptive self-defense, U.S.
advocacy of, 105, 118–119,
120–121

Private enterprise, UN suspicion of, 108
Production vs. distribution of wealth, 82–83
Public health programs, UN's, 76–77, 78

Rashid, Amer Muhammed, 51
Reform of UN
    author's approach, 110–121
    UN internal approach, 92–109
Regional alliances, 8, 11, 14, 91, 104
Regulatory agencies, success of UN, 75–80
Riad, Mahmoud, 22
Ridgway, Gen. Matthew, 17
Righter, Rosemary, 45–46, 57, 84, 93
Rikhye, Indar Jit, 21–22
Riza, Iqbal, 53–54
Roosevelt, Eleanor, 9
Roosevelt, Franklin Delano, 9–10
Rose, Gen. Michael, 26
Rossett, Claudia, 54–55
Rule of law, universal participation in, 107
Russia, 4–5, 86
    See also Soviet Union
Rwanda genocide (1990s)
    corruption in war crimes tribunal for, 46
    France's downplaying of, 85
    UN ineffectiveness in dealing with, 29–31
    and UN organizational self-interest, 58, 90
    U.S. lack of action on, 91

Salaries, UN, 43, 44–45

Sanctions/embargoes, 24, 25–26, 39–40, 48–56
SARS (Sudden Acute Respiratory Syndrome), 76
Saudi Arabia, lack of human rights criticism of, 60
Save the Children Fund, 46
Schlesinger, Stephen, 8
Secrecy of UN secretariat, 55, 87–88, 96–97
Secretariat, UN
    and efficiency reforms, 94–95
    oil-for-food program role, 54–55
    radical reform of, 113
    secrecy of operations, 55, 87–88, 96–97
    and self-interests of UN members, 89
Secretaries general, politics of, 58
    See also Annan, Kofi; Boutros-Ghali, Boutros
Security Council
    abolishment of, 113
    as control on U.S. expansionism, 3, 4
    failure to respond to human rights abuses, 60
    and freedoms of end of Cold War, 23
    inappropriate election of rogue members, 88–89
    ineffectiveness of, 18–19, 31–33
    and Iran's nuclear deceptions, 39–40
    and Korean War, 19–20
    and Kuwait crisis, 33–34
    monopoly on UN use of force, 9

oil-for-food program role,
54–55
as pillar of UN organization,
14
reassurance role in peacekeeping, 25, 33, 73–75
reform of, 100, 101–103,
106–109, 112
and Rwandan genocide,
29–31
self-serving nature of, 90
and Serb/Muslim conflict in
Yugoslavia, 23–24, 25–29
Somalia debacle, 29
on use of force, 1–2, 119, 120
U.S.'s sword-bearing role in,
112
Self-defense (Article 51), 9,
19–20, 105, 118–121
Self-interest, U.S.'s enlightened,
111
Self-interest of UN as paramount
principle, 89–91
Serbian/Bosnian conflict, 23–24,
25–29, 46, 85, 91
Sevan, Benon, 50, 51
Sexual exploitation by UN staff,
46
Sexual harassment by UNHCR,
47–48
Sierra Leone, peacekeeping in, 75
Sinai peninsula, Egyptian
demand for removal of UN
forces, 21–22
Sinecure system, UN staffing as,
44
Situation room establishment by
UN, 97
Six-Day War (1967), Arab-Israeli,
21–22

Smith, Gaddis, 15
Social and Economic Aspects of
Security Threats, 98–99
Socialism
and civil society idea, 99–100
and Non-Aligned Movement,
82–83
UN leaning toward, 69, 70–71,
108–109
Sokolski, Henry, 40
Somalia debacle (1990s), 29,
32–33, 74
Sovereignty, national, vs. civil
society idea, 100
Soviet Union
attitudes toward UN formation, 8–9
and ending of Cold War, 23
and Korean War, 19–20
and politics of Security Council membership, 18–19
U.S. misconceptions about,
12, 15–16
Specialized agencies, UN, 75–80,
112–113
Srebrenica, Serbian massacre at,
26–29
Stalin, Joseph, 8–9, 16
States rights vs. individual rights,
70–71
Stettinius, Edward, 9
Sudan and Darfur crisis, 60, 75,
83
Sudden Acute Respiratory Syndrome (SARS), 76
Supernumeraries, excessive numbers in UN, 94
Sutton Investments Ltd., 53
Syria, election to Security Council,
88–89

Tanzania and ineffectiveness of foreign aid, 71

Telecommunication regulation, UN's, 75–76

Terrorism
  need for universal definition, 107
  and preemptive self-defense, 120–121
  and UN's biases, 61, 64, 66–68

Thant, U, 22

Tharoor, Shashi, 4, 56–57, 79

Third World nations, 69–72, 81–83, 84, 101, 108–109

Thornburgh, Dick, 43, 94

Tito, Josep, 82

Totalitarian/dictatorial regimes, 84–85, 86
  See also China; Soviet Union

Tower of Babble: How the United Nations Has Created Global Chaos (Gold), 66–67

Transparency, UN's lack of, 87–88, 96–97

Tsunami of 2004, UN's lack of resources to respond to, 77–78

Tutsis, Hutu genocide of, 30–31

UN Commission on Human Rights, *see* Commission on Human Rights

UNCTAD (United Nations Conference on Trade and Development), 69

Undersecretaries general and UN inefficiency, 43

UNEF (United Nations Emergency Force), 21–22

UNESCO (United Nations Educational, Cultural and Scientific Organization), 70

UN High Commissioner for Refugees (UNHCR), 47–48

UNICEF, 76

Unipolarity and international concern about U.S. power, 5

United Kingdom, *see* Britain, Great

United Nations Conference on Trade and Development (UNCTAD), 69

United Nations Development Decade, 69

United Nations Educational, Cultural and Scientific Organization (UNESCO), 70

United Nations Emergency Force (UNEF), 21–22

United States
  and alliances, 11, 12, 110, 115, 117
  as creator of UN, 7–16
  democracies' resentment of, 103–104
  and ending of Cold War, 23
  fears of U.S. power, 2–4, 5, 15–16
  and future of Security Council, 106–109
  idealism about international organization, 1, 9, 12, 14
  internationalism vs. isolationism, 7, 10–11, 13
  as nation builder, 74
  as only real policeman on Security Council, 19
  peacekeeping contribution, 110–112

and Rwandan genocide, 30
voting records of UN members in relation to,
    123–129
Uniting for Peace, 20, 66
Unity, international, as illusion, 24
Universal Postal Union, 76
Universal vs. differential values,
    14–15, 24, 84
UN Protection Force (UNPROFOR) in Bosnia, 27–28
UN Relief and Works Agency for
    Palestine Refugee
    (UNRWA), 64

Values, universal vs. differential,
    14–15, 24, 84
Van Boven, Theo, 58
Vedrine, Hubert, 3
Veto, Security Council, reforms
    of, 112
Villepin, Dominique de, 4
Volcker Commission, 50–56
Vote-trading practices, 45, 88
Voting records, UN members vs.
    U.S., 123–129

War crimes tribunals, financial
    irregularities concerning,
    46
Washington, George, 115
Weapons of mass destruction,
    34–42, 105, 120
Wedgwood, Ruth, 44

Westexim (dummy firm), 52
WHO (World Health Organization), 45–46, 76, 78
Wilson, Michael, 51
Wilson, Woodrow, 7–8, 115
Wirth, Timothy, 77, 112
Wolfers, Arnold, 111
Women's rights and lack of criticism for fundamentalist
    Islamic regimes, 60
World Bank, 101
World Conference Against
    Racism, 100
World Food Program, 77
World government
    and demise of nationalism, 80
    and democracy, 99–100
    and reform of UN, 93
    UN as skeleton for, 14
    as unnecessary evil, 113
World Health Organization
    (WHO), 45–46, 76, 78
World War I and gestation of UN,
    7–8, 10
World War II and gestation of
    UN, 8–9, 12–13

Yeselson, Abraham, 23
Yugoslavia, Serbian/Bosnian conflict, 23–24, 25–29, 46, 85,
    91

Ziegler, Jean, 78
Zionism, UN bias against, 65

About the Author

Joshua Muravchik is a resident scholar at the American Enterprise Institute. He is the author of eight books and hundreds of articles that have appeared in numerous magazines and every major American daily, ranging over the fields of U.S. foreign policy, international relations, American politics, history, political theory, and media criticism. He holds a doctorate in government from Georgetown University and serves as an adjunct professor at the Institute of World Politics, an adjunct scholar at the Washington Institute for Near East Policy, and a member of the editorial boards of *The Journal of Democracy* and *World Affairs*. In 1986 the *Wall Street Journal* wrote that "Joshua Muravchik may be the most cogent and careful of the neoconservative writers on foreign policy." His book *Heaven on Earth: The Rise and Fall of Socialism* (Encounter Books, 2002), selected by *Choice* as one of the Outstanding Academic Titles of 2002, was released by PBS in 2005 as a documentary miniseries. His latest book, *Covering the Intifada: How the Media Reported the Palestinian Uprising,* was published in 2003 by the Washington Institute for Near East Policy.